P9-DMZ-473

NORTH PORT PUBLIC LIBRARY

JUL 0 3 2014

13800 S. TAMIAMI TRAIL
NORTH PORT, FL 34287

31969022191216

Ryan Gosling

by Cherese Cartlidge

NORTH PORT PUBLIC LIBRARY

13800 S. TAMIAMI TRAIL
NORTH PORT, FL 34287

LUCENT BOOKS

A part of Gale, Cengage Learning

GALE
CENGAGE Learning·

Farmington Hills, Mich • San Francisco • New York • Waterville, Maine
Meriden, Conn • Mason, Ohio • Chicago

GALE
CENGAGE Learning·

© 2014 Gale, Cengage Learning

WCN:01-100-101

ALL RIGHTS RESERVED. No part of this work covered by the copyright herein may be reproduced, transmitted, stored, or used in any form or by any means graphic, electronic, or mechanical, including but not limited to photocopying, recording, scanning, digitizing, taping, Web distribution, information networks, or information storage and retrieval systems, except as permitted under Section 107 or 108 of the 1976 United States Copyright Act, without the prior written permission of the publisher.

Every effort has been made to trace the owners of copyrighted material.

LIBRARY OF CONGRESS CATALOGING-IN-PUBLICATION DATA

Cartlidge, Cherese.
 Ryan Gosling / by Cherese Cartlidge.
    pages cm. -- (People in the news)
 Includes bibliographical references and index.
 ISBN 978-1-4205-0890-1 (hardcover)
 1. Gosling, Ryan, 1980---Juvenile literature. 2. Actors--United States--Biography--Juvenile literature. I. Title.
 PN2287.G643C37 2013
 791.4302'8092--dc23
 [B]
                                                        2014003667

Lucent Books
27500 Drake Rd.
Farmington Hills, MI 48331

ISBN-13: 978-1-4205-0890-1
ISBN-10: 1-4205-0890-3

Printed in the United States of America
1 2 3 4 5 6 7 18 17 16 15 14

Contents

Fame and celebrity are alluring. People are drawn to those who walk in fame's spotlight, whether they are known for great accomplishments or for notorious deeds. The lives of the famous pique public interest and attract attention, perhaps because their experiences seem in some ways so different from, yet in other ways so similar to, our own.

Newspapers, magazines, and television regularly capitalize on this fascination with celebrity by running profiles of famous people. For example, television programs such as *Entertainment Tonight* devote all their programming to stories about entertainment and entertainers. Magazines such as People fill their pages with stories of the private lives of famous people. Even newspapers, newsmagazines, and television news frequently delve into the lives of well-known personalities. Despite the number of articles and programs, few provide more than a superficial glimpse at their subjects.

Lucent's People in the News series offers young readers a deeper look into the lives of today's newsmakers, the influences that have shaped them, and the impact they have had in their fields of endeavor and on other people's lives. The subjects of the series hail from many disciplines and walks of life. They include authors, musicians, athletes, political leaders, entertainers, entrepreneurs, and others who have made a mark on modern life and who, in many cases, will continue to do so for years to come.

These biographies are more than factual chronicles. Each book emphasizes the contributions, accomplishments, or deeds that have brought fame or notoriety to the individual and shows how that person has influenced modern life. Authors portray their subjects in a realistic, unsentimental light. For example, Bill Gates—cofounder of the software giant Microsoft—has been instrumental in making personal computers the most vital tool of the modern age. Few dispute his business savvy, his perseverance, or his technical expertise, yet critics say he is ruthless in his dealings with competitors and driven more by his desire to maintain Microsoft's dominance in the computer industry than by an interest in furthering technology.

In these books, young readers will encounter inspiring stories about real people who achieved success despite enormous obstacles. Oprah Winfrey—one of the most powerful, most watched, and wealthiest women in television history—spent the first six years of her life in the care of her grandparents while her unwed mother sought work and a better life elsewhere. Her adolescence was colored by pregnancy at age fourteen, rape, and sexual abuse.

Each author documents and supports his or her work with an array of primary and secondary source quotations taken from diaries, letters, speeches, and interviews. All quotes are footnoted to show readers exactly how and where biographers derive their information and provide guidance for further research. The quotations enliven the text by giving readers eyewitness views of the life and accomplishments of each person covered in the People in the News series.

In addition, each book in the series includes photographs, annotated bibliographies, timelines, and comprehensive indexes. For both the casual reader and the student researcher, the People in the News series offers insight into the lives of today's newsmakers—people who shape the way we live, work, and play in the modern age.

The Secret to His Success

Ryan Gosling is one of the most respected and sought-after actors in Hollywood. Ruben Fleischer, who directed him in the 2013 action film *Gangster Squad*, attributes Gosling's success to the fact that he is "funny and charming. . . . He has a magnetic quality—larger than life."[1] The *New York Times* describes him as simply "disarming."[2] And as one writer for the Associated Press pointed out, "The guy ain't bad looking."[3] Certainly all of these qualities contribute to the making of a successful movie star. Yet the secret to Gosling's success is something more; it lies in large part in his ability to totally immerse himself in a role, believably becoming the character.

Plunging In

Time and again, Gosling has plunged himself into a role. For example, to prepare for his role as Noah Calhoun in the 2004 romantic drama *The Notebook*, he worked as a furniture maker's apprentice. In fact, Gosling made the dining room table and some of the other furniture that is shown in the movie. In the action-packed 2011 crime drama *Drive*, Gosling performed as many of his own stunts as the movie's producers would allow him to. He also spent hours taking apart the movie's 1973 Chevy Malibu and painstakingly putting it back together again to prepare for his role as a mechanic and stuntman. For his Oscar-nominated performance as a drug-addicted teacher in *Half Nelson* (2006), he spent days shadowing a history teacher in a Brooklyn middle school.

One of the quirkiest movies Gosling has starred in is *Lars and the Real Girl* (2007), in which his character falls in love with a life-size plastic doll named Bianca. Gosling underwent an intense experience in order to prepare for his role as the sweet, socially inept Lars and be able to do a convincing job of being in love with an inanimate object. For an entire month, Gosling lived with the doll in the basement of his mother's house in Ontario, Canada. He talked to her and ate meals sitting at a table with her. "My poor mother, she doesn't ask questions any more," Gosling says. "She just says, 'Oh yeah . . . [the] doll movie.'"[4] Gosling's dedication to his craft paid off: He was nominated for a Golden Globe for his performance in the film.

Ryan Gosling truly becomes involved in the roles he plays in his movies. For the movie Drive, *Gosling did many of his own stunts and worked on the car in the movie to portray his mechanic/stunt driver character as realistically as possible.*

Building a Castle

Gosling put himself through another thorough preparation process for his role in the 2010 bittersweet romantic drama *Blue Valentine*, in which he starred opposite Michelle Williams. He and Williams lived together in a house in Scranton, Pennsylvania, for a month before shooting began. The director had them live just like their characters in the movie would—doing chores, buying groceries, following a budget, even hanging out with the little girl who would play their daughter in the film. "It was just Michelle and I baking birthday cakes and having fake birthdays and Christmas and wrapping presents and cleaning the house and fighting, just living in this house,"[5] Gosling ex-

Ryan Gosling and Michelle Williams in a scene from the 2010 movie Blue Valentine. *The two lived together in the same house for a month to get to know each other well enough to make their on-screen marriage more believable to the audience.*

plains. This intense experience of being thrown together began to mimic the everyday reality of an actual marriage, with all its ups and downs. "We fought all day, and then we'd have to take [our characters' daughter] Faith to the family fun park," Gosling says, "whatever we could do to create real memories, so when it came time to shoot the . . . film, we were drawing on real memories."[6]

This feeling of reality continued during the actual filming, and there were times that everything felt so real that Gosling actually forgot he was in a movie. The lines between "reality" and "movie" became blurred on several occasions, such as the time he fell asleep on the couch during a lull in filming. When he awoke he discovered that the director had continued filming while Gosling slept and Williams cleaned up the house around him.

As with *Lars and the Real Girl*, Gosling's immersion in his character for *Blue Valentine* was so deep that it was difficult for him to pull himself out of the character when the project came to a close. "Michelle and I found it hard to take off our wedding bands when it was over," he says. "We'd built this castle and then had to tear it down."[7] But again, his dedication was rewarded; he received his second Golden Globe nomination for his work in *Blue Valentine*.

Everything Comes from the Inside

Gosling's ability to morph into one character after another has impressed audiences and directors alike. Derek Cianfrance, who directed him in both *Blue Valentine* and 2013's *The Place Beyond the Pines*, points out that Gosling approaches every role he plays by transforming himself into the character. "When Ryan gets to live these other lives, he lives them fully and doesn't leave anything behind,"[8] Cianfrance explains.

But the true secret to Gosling's success may be something else. It is not so much that he can become someone else for a role but rather that he reaches deep inside himself to pull these various characters to the surface. Time and again, he has pulled out of himself what he needs to in order to play these varied characters. "I don't become characters," Gosling explains. "They're all me."[9]

Chapter 1

The Road to Disney World

Ryan Gosling grew up in a family that moved around a lot, usually because of his father's job. This created a lot of instability that affected Ryan's formative years. He had a hard time making friends, and he was so hyperactive that he had trouble sitting still and paying attention in school. In addition, his parents divorced when he was very young. But Ryan's childhood was far from unhappy, thanks to the loving support and encouragement of his devoted mother.

"A Great Place to Grow Up"

On November 12, 1980, Thomas and Donna Gosling welcomed their second child: a blue-eyed, blond-haired boy they named Ryan Thomas. Baby Ryan was also welcomed home from St. Joseph's Hospital by his sister, Mandi, who was four years old. The Goslings lived in London, a city in the Canadian province of Ontario. But the family moved several times after Ryan was born and eventually settled in Cornwall, Ontario, where Ryan and Mandi spent their early childhood.

The Goslings were a working-class family. Ryan's father and uncle both worked at the Domtar paper mill in Cornwall. Ryan's father was a traveling salesman for the mill, so he was frequently away from home. Ryan's mother worked as a secretary. The Gosling family often struggled to make ends meet. Years later, Ryan admitted that while growing up, he had "this thing about money. . . . Anybody who had it I didn't like, 'cause I didn't have it."[10]

Despite not having much money, Ryan liked living in Canada. He particularly liked Cornwall—despite the rotten-egg smell from the paper mill that permeated the air. The industrial Cornwall had a population of roughly forty thousand at the time, and Ryan liked its multiculturalism. Although small, it is only about an hour away from Montreal, which is the second-largest city in Canada. French is the official language in Montreal and is spoken as a first language by well over half the residents. In Cornwall, about a quarter of the residents speak French as their first language. Ryan's father is of French Canadian descent, and

An aerial view of downtown Cornwall, Ontario, Canada, where Gosling spent his preteen years.

the Gosling children grew up hearing both English and French spoken every day. Today, although Ryan does understand some French, he is not fluent himself.

A Religious Upbringing

Religion was a big part of the Goslings' lives and had an important influence on Ryan growing up. He says he and his sister "were brought up pretty religious" and explains that his parents were devout Mormons. "It was a part of everything—what they ate, how they thought,"[11] he explains.

A Mormon temple in Salt Lake City, Utah. Gosling was raised in the Mormon Church, which he credits for some of his social skills, including his manners and performing in public.

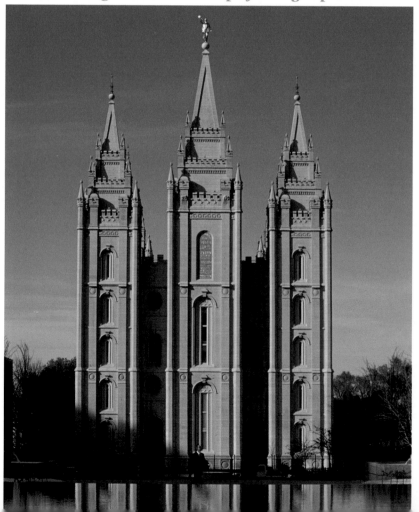

Despite the fact that his parents were both religious and raised their children in the Mormon faith, Ryan did not share their beliefs. When he was about twelve years old, he confessed to his mother that he did not embrace Mormonism the way she did. He greatly appreciated that his mother respected his right to come to his own understanding of things. "This is an option, but this isn't the only option," she said to him. "This is an idea, but this isn't the only idea. You have to find your own truth."[12]

Even though he did not consider himself a Mormon, he recognizes the important role that his parents' religion played in his life. He credits his religious upbringing with helping to socialize him through meeting people in church, shaking hands, and speaking and singing in public. He also learned to be respectful and polite toward others, as well as to accept views that differed from his own.

Here Comes Trouble

When Ryan was growing up, his father was not around much because he traveled often for his job. Even when he was home, he was not very involved with the children, so Donna raised Ryan and Mandi virtually by herself. This was no easy task, particularly when it came to Ryan. As he progressed from baby to toddler to preschooler, he became increasingly difficult to keep up with. "He was like an escape artist. He'd run out of the house naked," Donna recalls. She would tell the other kids on the block, "If you see Ryan, don't come get me. Sit on him and send someone else."[13]

Ryan and Mandi's childhoods were often disrupted because the family moved around a lot, even after relocating to Cornwall. In fact, one move came about because Donna was convinced that the house they were living in was haunted. The frequent moves were difficult for Ryan. Once he started school, he often felt as though he did not fit in, and he had a hard time forming lasting friendships with other kids. "I had no pals," he recalls, "none."[14]

Ryan also had problems keeping up with his schoolwork. Always a very active child, he had a hard time staying in his seat and frequently got into trouble for not paying attention in class. Not surprisingly, he struggled academically and came to believe that he was not very smart. Even though he kept advancing to the next grade each year, Ryan knew there were things he could not do that he should have been able to do—such as read. This led to problems for him, as he explains: "When you're in class and you can't read and everyone else can, it's pretty frustrating. I couldn't absorb any of the information, so I caused trouble."[15]

One incident in first grade led to Ryan's being suspended. He had just seen the 1982 Sylvester Stallone action movie *Rambo: First Blood*, which left a huge impression on him. "I thought I was Rambo,"[16] he says. His belief that he actually was the action hero from the movie had serious repercussions, as he explains: "I filled my Fisher-Price Houdini kit with steak knives and brought them to school and started throwing them at kids at recess. I got suspended and my parents nixed R-rated movies."[17]

A Year at Home

Ryan's troubles escalated as he progressed through elementary school. A scrawny kid with few friends and a penchant for troublemaking, he soon became the target of schoolyard bullies. As a result, he got into frequent fights and was often sent to the principal's office. And as the bullying and fighting intensified, he fell further and further behind in school. These were difficult years for him. "I hated being a kid," he says. "I didn't like being told what to do, I didn't like my body, I didn't like any of it."[18]

Ryan's mother was very concerned about both his education and his physical safety. When the school recommended he be placed in a special-education class because he could not read, Donna decided to take things into her own hands. She pulled her ten-year-old son out of school to teach him herself.

Ryan had always felt the need to move around as he learned, something that was not usually allowed in school. But during the year his mother homeschooled him, he was encouraged to get up and walk around all he wanted to while she talked to him. Donna also took a very creative approach to teaching him: She used rolls of paper from the paper mill to cover the walls of

Ryan Gosling's mother, Donna (left), raised him for the most part on her own. When Gosling failed to learn to read in school, she homeschooled him for a year to help him catch up.

their basement and had Ryan draw all over them as he processed what he was learning. "If I was learning about history, I would draw the scenarios that I was learning about or the people that she was telling me about. And I was able to remember them that way,"[19] he explains. The bond between Ryan and his mother grew even deeper during that year as the two of them watched old movies, listened to music, and talked about life.

Movies, Music, and Muppets

One of the things Ryan liked best about his childhood—and which left an indelible mark on him—was watching movies on TV with his mom. But it was not only movies with action stars such as Arnold Schwarzenegger and Sylvester Stallone that made a strong impression on him. One of his favorite movies was the 1955 classic film *East of Eden*, starring screen icon James Dean. Other favorite films included the 1986 mystery *Blue Velvet* and the 1987 coming-of-age drama *Dirty Dancing*. Ryan also enjoyed comedies, and he watched a lot of Abbott and Costello movies as a child. Bud Abbott and Lou Costello were an American comedy team who appeared in dozens of movies during the 1940s and 1950s.

One actor in particular had a big influence on him: legendary tough guy Marlon Brando, whose award-winning film career began in 1950. He particularly liked Brando's distinctive way of talking, which was often almost a mumble. Gosling relates, "As a kid I decided that a Canadian accent doesn't sound tough. I thought guys should sound like Marlon Brando."[20] So he started imitating the way Brando talked in order to sound tough and to change his own accent (and he still talks this way today).

Other early influences on him included musicians as well as actors. Billy Idol, a 1980s British punk rock sensation, was a particular favorite. He especially liked the videos to Idol's hit songs "Rebel Yell" and "Dancing with Myself," and he would sing and dance along with the videos, strutting and boxing the air in imitation of the moves Idol made.

One of Ryan's favorite TV shows when he was growing up was *The Muppet Show*. In fact, it was an episode of this show that helped inspire him to become an actor. When he saw actress Raquel Welch on the show, dancing with a furry spider, he quickly developed his first crush. He wondered how he could possibly meet her, and then he came to a life-changing conclusion: "Well, she's on TV, so to meet her I have to get on TV myself."[21]

"Elvis Perry Security"

As a child Ryan was already taking steps toward his goal of getting on TV. He first gained experience as a performer by taking

Ryan Gosling credits his sister Mandi for helping raise him as a child. The two also performed together at weddings.

ballet classes and dancing in recitals while he was in elementary school. He also started performing along with his sister when he was about eight years old. The two of them sang at local weddings; while the bride sat in a chair, Ryan would get down on his knees and sing "When a Man Loves a Woman" to her just before the garter ceremony (at which, during the wedding reception, the bridegroom removes one of the bride's garters that hold up her stockings and throws it to a waiting group of bachelors). Afterward Mandi would sing a song, then the two of them would sing Bob Seger's "Old Time Rock and Roll" and sometimes, for a finale, Ryan would sing 1960s' teen idol Dion's "Runaround Sue."

Ryan and Mandi also performed in local talent shows, including one at their church in 1991. The two of them sang "Gonna Make You Sweat (Everybody Dance Now)," a hit song by C+C Music Factory that spawned a dance craze across the nation in the early 1990s. Although Ryan was only ten years old at the time, the dance-off duet he performed with Mandi—which culminated with her leaping into his arms—wowed the audience in the auditorium.

Ryan's close relationship with his sister was an important early influence on him, and he idolized her. "My sister was my best friend and my hero growing up,"[22] he says. The strong bond between them was evident each time the two of them performed together onstage. Ryan admits that as a kid, he had a strong desire "to always do the things that she wanted to do, and impress her. . . . I was kind of showing off."[23]

Another family member also played a part in bringing Ryan closer to his goal of becoming an actor: his uncle Perry, who lived in the Goslings' basement for several years. Perry was an Elvis Presley impersonator, and Ryan's experience as a wedding singer helped him land a spot performing with his uncle, who billed himself as Elvis Perry. "He looked nothing like Elvis. He was bald, had a mustache and a big birthmark," Ryan recalls. He used to watch his uncle, who made his own costumes, prepare for a show and was fascinated by the transformation. When Perry went onstage, he not only sounded just like Elvis, he became Elvis—and this had a profound effect on Ryan. "There was something about watching him kind of get into character that really made an impression on me,"[24] Ryan recalls.

Ryan did not do much actual performing onstage with his uncle. In fact, his job title was head of security—and he took his position very seriously. He wore a gold lamé jacket that said "Elvis Perry Security" on the back. When his uncle would take scarves from his neck to hand to women in the audience, it was

Keeping the "King" Alive

When Ryan Gosling was a child, his uncle performed as an impersonator of the late Elvis Presley, a superstar who was called the King of Rock 'n' Roll. Entertainers began impersonating Presley as far back as the 1950s, but after his death in 1977 the phenomenon boomed. Even today, more than three decades later, Elvis impersonators (known as tribute artists) are still popular not only in the United States but in other countries as well. In fact, there are tens of thousands of them, as Susan Doll, author of the book *Elvis for Dummies*, writes: "It's nearly impossible to accurately calculate the number of Elvis tribute artists throughout the world, but estimates range from 10,000 to 250,000."

As popular as they are, though, Elvis tribute artists are also the target of criticism. Many people, especially those in the media, ridicule entertainers who get onstage dressed as the iconic King, imitate his gestures, and croon his famous songs. But for those who enjoy watching these artists perform, it is all about reliving wonderful memories. "Fans don't expect impersonators to take Elvis's place," says Doll. "They enjoy them as a way to remember and relive one of Elvis's live performances."

Susan Doll. *Elvis for Dummies*. Hoboken, NJ: Wiley, 2009, p. 273.

Ryan's job to hand him new scarves. He also handed his uncle teddy bears to throw to the audience when Perry sang Elvis's song "Teddy Bear."

Joining the Mouseketeers

Even though Ryan did not do much in the way of performing with the Elvis Perry act, he did gain valuable experience in putting on a show and being in front of an audience. By the time he was twelve years old, he had his first agent, who encouraged him to attend an audition for the variety series *The All New Mickey Mouse Club* on the Disney Channel. Aimed at tweens and young teens, this revival of the original 1950s series was holding open auditions in Montreal in January 1993. Although he had no formal acting training, Ryan joined some seventeen thousand other hopefuls in a rigorous audition process that included singing, dancing, and acting.

When Ryan learned he had won one of the seven new spots on the show, he was thrilled. "I hit the roof," he said. "My mother and I, we were just like jumping around . . . It was amazing."[25] That spring Ryan moved with his mother and sister—as well as the other cast members—to Orlando, Florida, where the show would be taped. Because all of the Mouseketeers were school aged, there was a tutor on the set who helped them with assignments from their regular schools back home.

As teens, Ryan Gosling and Britney Spears joined the cast of **The All New Mickey Mouse Club.**

Ryan's initial excitement over being cast in the show soon began to dim, however. He was a member of a cast that included future stars Christina Aguilera, JC Chasez, Keri Russell, Britney Spears, and Justin Timberlake. Although Ryan was certainly talented, it soon became obvious that he was out of his league compared with his fellow cast mates. He admits that he probably passed the audition because of his bold confidence rather than pure talent. Because of this, Ryan wound up not being featured on the show as much as the other kids were. He would sing and dance with the others at the beginning and end of the show and occasionally appear in a sketch. "I didn't end up working that much, which was disheartening,"[26] he recalls.

Another serious blow came just as Ryan was getting started on the show: His parents decided to divorce. Because of this, Ryan's mother could not afford for them to live in the same apartment complex as the other cast members and their families. So Ryan, Donna, and Mandi lived in the nearby Yogi Bear Trailer Park instead. This, in addition to the fact that he was the only Mouseketeer from Canada, set him apart from the other cast members.

Ryan's father had been largely absent from his life, even before his parents decided to divorce. So early on Donna had taken over the role of being a father to her son—and Mandi often filled in as a mother for him. "I was literally raised by my mother and my sister,"[27] Gosling recalls. Eventually, however, Donna and Mandi had to return to Canada so his mom could deal with the divorce proceedings. So Ryan lived for six months with Justin Timberlake and his mother, who became Ryan's temporary legal guardian.

Playing at Disney World

Because Ryan did not work as much as the other cast members did, he had a lot of free time on his hands. He spent most of it walking around Disney World and riding on the rides. The theme park made a big impression on Ryan. He especially loved the Haunted Mansion ride and would go on it whenever he was not working on the show. He saw many other intriguing sights,

A Place of Magic

Walt Disney World opened in Lake Buena Vista, Florida, near Orlando, in October 1971. Its Magic Kingdom park was modeled after the original Disneyland but was far more elaborate and much larger than the Anaheim, California, park. In the years since its opening, Disney World has grown into an enormous resort that captivates and delights millions of visitors from all over the world. Today it boasts four theme parks, two water parks, twenty-five resort hotels, five golf courses, and the ESPN Wide World of Sports Complex.

The two years that Ryan Gosling spent in Florida as part of *The All New Mickey Mouse Club* were among the happiest years of his life. He has referred to it as a magical time, and a great deal of the magic was because of the opportunity to hang out at the nearby Walt Disney World whenever he was not working. He was fascinated by all that the great Walt Disney had created solely on the basis of his dreams, and the young Gosling fantasized about believing so strongly in his own dreams someday. "It changed my life, you know," he says. "Disney World the park changed my life more than the experience of making that show."

Quoted in NPR. "Ryan Gosling: Fully Immersed in *Blue Valentine*." Transcript, December 15, 2010. www.wbur.org/npr/131963261/ryan-gosling-fully-immersed-in-blue-valentine.

Gosling lived in Orlando, Florida, during his years on The All New Mickey Mouse Club. *He often spent his days at Disney World, where he enjoyed an insider's view of the park.*

too. "It was interesting as a kid to go backstage to the commissary, and to see all of the people who were playing the characters with their heads off next to them while they were eating lunch,"[28] he remembers.

Ryan and Justin became close friends, and they had their share of adventures together, too. On several occasions, the two of them "borrowed" a golf cart from the back lot of the studio and drove over to the nearby MGM Studio in Orlando, where they bought milkshakes.

At other times they wandered the park together at night and would sometimes sneak into Pleasure Island, an area of Disney World that contained nightclubs for adult visitors.

Even though things had not worked out quite the way he had hoped, Ryan was making the best of his time in Florida. When *The All New Mickey Mouse Club* was canceled in 1995, he rejoined his mother and sister in Canada, bringing with him fond memories of his time in Orlando. He still thinks of his time in Florida as "the greatest two years ever."[29] Now, as he returned to Canada, he hoped he would be able to find more work on TV so he could continue to pursue his dream of becoming an actor.

Chapter 2

Making a Name for Himself

Ryan Gosling continued to pursue acting after moving back to Canada in 1995. He began with guest spots on several Canadian or joint Canadian-American family TV shows before landing permanent spots on two TV series. These would lead to bigger and better things for him by the time he was in his late teens.

The Family Breadwinner

Ryan landed his first gig only a few months after returning to Canada. It was a guest spot on the TV series *Are You Afraid of the Dark?* The show, a favorite of Ryan's, was filmed in Canada and aired in both Canada and the United States. The original series ran from 1990 to 1996. The show featured mildly scary stories that were geared toward children and teens. During each episode, a group of kids would sit around a campfire while one of them told the others a story with a scary, supernatural, or fantasy theme. Viewers watched the story being acted out by that week's guest stars. Ryan appeared in a 1995 episode titled "The Tale of Station 109.1." He played a boy who locked his death-obsessed younger brother in a hearse as a practical joke and wound up having to rescue him after the boy was mistaken for a dead body and nearly sent to the afterlife.

Following his spot on *Are You Afraid of the Dark?*, Ryan landed a string of guest-starring roles in other family TV shows. In 1996 he appeared on several different shows, including the very first episode of the Canadian science-fiction drama *Psi Factor: Chronicles of the Paranormal*, which was narrated by fellow Canadian actor Dan Aykroyd of *Saturday Night Live* fame. Ryan next appeared in an episode of *Kung Fu: The Legend Continues* (a sequel to the 1970s TV series *Kung Fu*, starring David Carradine), which was filmed in Toronto, Ontario.

Ryan continued to appear in Canadian productions throughout that year. He had a guest spot on the highly acclaimed series *Road to Avonlea*, also filmed in Ontario. Set in the early 1900s, the series was based on the classic children's books by Lucy Maud Montgomery. Throughout the show's seven seasons, a number of well-known actors made guest appearances, including Faye Dunaway, Christopher Reeve, Meg Tilly, and Treat Williams, among many others.

Other television shows that Ryan appeared in that year included an episode of *Goosebumps*, a children's spooky show

In 1996 Ryan Gosling guest starred in an episode of Road to Avonlea, *a popular Canadian TV series that starred actress Sarah Polley (far right).*

based on the series of books of the same title by R.L. Stine. The episode, titled "Say Cheese and Die," was based on the volume of the same title in the book series. Ryan also appeared in the very first episode of *The Adventures of Shirley Holmes*, a Canadian mystery series. The show's title character, Shirley Holmes, was the great grand-niece of fictional detective Sherlock Holmes. Ryan appeared in the episode titled "The Case of the Burning Building." He also had a recurring role as Scott Stuckey in two episodes during the first season of *Flash Forward*, a series for tweens and teens created by the Disney Channel.

Ryan finished out 1996 by appearing on the teen drama series *Ready or Not* in an episode titled "I Do, I Don't." Part of the reason Ryan took on so many roles was that his mother was no longer working, so he had become the family breadwinner. By age sixteen, he says, "I was working for the money because that was the only thing taking care of us at that point, the shows that I was doing."[30]

The Dropout Plays a High School Student

During his first two years back in Canada, Ryan appeared in one guest-starring TV role after another. He also continued his education by going back to school. He first attended Cornwall Collegiate and Vocational High School, where his favorite classes were drama and fine arts. By the time he was sixteen, he and his mother and sister had moved to Burlington, Ontario, where he attended Lester B. Pearson High School. Although the year of homeschooling with his mother had boosted his self-esteem, Ryan still did not perform well academically. He took a hard look at his life and came to an important realization. "I didn't want to work in a paper mill, and I wasn't going to stay in school,"[31] he explains. So in 1997, when he was sixteen years old, Ryan decided to drop out of high school to focus on his acting career. In fact, Ryan, his mother, and his sister all agreed as a family to put Ryan's career first.

Although no longer a high school student, Ryan's next job was, ironically, playing a high school student. After two years

Ryan Gosling (second from right) played the role of Alan Bosley in the 2000 movie Remember the Titans.

of guest starring, he became a regular cast member in the teen comedy-drama series *Breaker High*, which ran from 1997 to 1998. It ran for only one season, showing in both Canada and the United States. It was filmed entirely in British Columbia, Canada, but was set in a high school on a cruise ship. Ryan played Sean Hanlon, a wannabe ladies' man, and appeared in all forty-four episodes of the series.

While appearing on *Breaker High*, Ryan also got a couple of bit parts in movies. In the 1997 Canadian production *Frankenstein and Me*, he played one of a group of teens who stumbles upon the real Frankenstein's monster and tries to bring it back to life. Ryan loved working on the film and learning about classic horror productions that the characters in the film were

The Magnificence of New Zealand

When Ryan Gosling was seventeen years old, he moved to New Zealand to star in the television series *Young Hercules*. A few years later *The Lord of the Rings: The Fellowship of the Ring* (2001) was filmed there, as were its two sequels. These were followed by other blockbuster films such as *The Chronicles of Narnia: The Lion, the Witch and the Wardrobe* (2005) and *The Hobbit: An Unexpected Journey* (2012). These movies have given filmgoers worldwide a chance to see some of the most beautiful scenery on earth, including ice-age glaciers, rugged mountains, meandering rivers, crystal-clear lakes, and ancient forests. Andrew Adamson, who directed *The Lion, the Witch and the Wardrobe*, says that New Zealand offers scenery that is rare and unspoiled. "There's very few places left in the world where you can point the camera and not see houses or hotels for 270 degrees in the frame," he says.

New Zealand is irresistible to filmmakers for other reasons as well, such as a large pool of affordable labor and highly talented workers. Also, groups such as the New Zealand Film Commission and Film New Zealand combine government funds with numerous incentives that are extremely attractive to filmmakers worldwide. For these reasons, along with unparalleled natural beauty, New Zealand has become one of the world's most popular filmmaking locations.

Quoted in Tourism New Zealand. "New Zealand's Film Star Landscapes." www.new zealand.com/travel/media/features/film&television/film_new-zealand-perfect-backdrop .cfm.

interested in, such as the now-classic 1960s gothic soap opera *Dark Shadows*.

Ryan's work in *Frankenstein and Me* garnered him some positive attention. The Canadian horror magazine *Rue Morgue* noted that Ryan showed genuine "screen presence"[32] in his first movie role. The director of the film, Robert Tinnell, was likewise impressed:

Ryan was a very charismatic kid—and a very, very nice kid. They all were. He was so charismatic that I couldn't entertain the notion of him as the lead because I didn't think people would buy him as having the troubles that character endured. . . . Ryan threw himself into it. He was a little older than the others in the cast and emerged as a leader. Those kids just loved each other.[33]

Ryan next costarred in the 1998 TV movie *Nothing Too Good for a Cowboy*. This romantic western was filmed in Ontario. The movie was not widely viewed, and Ryan only had a small part in it. But his continued appearances in TV shows and movies were beginning to earn him the notice of casting directors. By 1998 Ryan's acting chops and hard work were about to pay off in a big way.

"Fake Tan, Leather Pants"

Ryan's first big break came at age seventeen, when he was cast in the title role of the Fox Kids TV series *Young Hercules*. The show was a spinoff of the 1990s TV series *Hercules: The Legendary Journeys*, starring Kevin Sorbo. *Young Hercules* was filmed in New Zealand, and Ryan lived in Auckland, the island nation's biggest city, for two years while working on the show. It was the first time he had ever lived on his own, and he loved it. To train for his role on the action-adventure series, Ryan underwent intensive martial arts training, including kung fu instruction. The training not only helped Ryan prepare for the physical demands of the part, it also helped boost his self-confidence in other areas of life.

By this time, Ryan was already approaching his full adult height of six feet. Yet although the physical training helped develop his strength, he still had a very long and thin physique. This posed a challenge for the wardrobe and makeup departments, which were tasked with making him look bulkier than he was. The original costume design was revamped to make his tunic broader in the chest and shoulders, and a lighter color of fabric was used to help make him look bigger. To aid in this illusion, makeup was applied to his arms to create the look of bigger muscles.

Ryan enjoyed his time in New Zealand. During the two years he lived there, he occasionally was able to visit nearby Australia. In many ways, his work on the show felt like a vacation to him. He took a lighthearted approach to the filming, regarding it more as play than work. He tried not to take himself too seriously in his role and said his goal was to "try and make the best show that we can, for kids to go away after school and just forget about homework and all that stuff."[34] Many aspects of the role made it a fun one to play. "I had a fake tan, leather pants," he said. "I was fighting imaginary monsters—they weren't really there [that is, they were computer generated and inserted into the scenes later], but I was acting like they were there."[35]

In the end, fifty episodes of *Young Hercules* were filmed, and Ryan appeared in all of them. The show ran for one season, from 1998 to 1999. Although the ratings were good, the network decided not to renew it for a second season. So Ryan found himself once again looking for work.

Act for Passion, Not a Paycheck

Ryan was almost nineteen years old by the time *Young Hercules* was canceled. He had primarily been working to help support his family, and thus he often took jobs that offered good paychecks rather than ones that featured characters he was passionate about playing. When *Young Hercules* ended and Ryan began searching for his next role, his mother said something that inspired him. She told him, "Don't take another job for money again."[36] She said that he had done enough to help support his family, and now it was time for him to be more selective and only take roles because he truly wanted to play them.

What Ryan wanted to play was a wider variety of roles. He also wanted to break out of being a child actor and be taken more seriously. So he made two big decisions. He decided not to do any more TV work and to instead focus solely on working in films. He also decided to move to Los Angeles. It had been his lifelong dream to go to Los Angeles and become an actor.

When he was a kid he used to tell himself, "I'm moving to California as soon as I can drive."[37] So, in 1999, Ryan made his way to Los Angeles, found an apartment, and started going out on auditions.

Working with His Idol

Although Ryan had decided not to take any more TV roles when he moved to Los Angeles, he changed his mind when he had the chance to work with comedian and actor Steve Carell, who had been one of Ryan's favorite performers for several years. Ryan auditioned and received the role in a TV pilot called *The Unbelievables*, about a family of retired superheroes. Besides Carell, the pilot featured veteran actors Corbin Bernsen and Tim Curry.

Ryan thoroughly enjoyed working with Carell. He also relished the opportunity to learn more about performing by observing one of his idols in action. "I would go to [the] set to watch him work," Ryan recalls. "One time he was so funny, the

Gosling met comedian and actor Steve Carell (right) while working on the TV series The Unbelievables. *Carell would work with Gosling again in the film* Crazy, Stupid, Love.

A Giant Leap

For many young people, the idea of appearing in movies, associating with famous stars, and being called a celebrity is something that only happens in dreams. Many imagine the lives of child stars to be packed from morning until night with fun, glamour, and excitement. To some extent that may be true. But when these stars grow up, Hollywood does not necessarily want them anymore—and that can be a devastating and cruel discovery for any young person. The unfortunate reality is that most child stars do not succeed at becoming adult stars, and many develop serious problems as a result.

Ryan Gosling is one of the rare celebrities who was able to make the transition from child star to adult star. But even though he was fortunate (and talented) enough to do so, Gosling knows from personal experience how tough it is. "It's hard to make the jump from being a child actor to an adult actor because it's hard to change people's perceptions of you," he says. "It was very difficult." Gosling is also blunt about the difficulties child stars face and says that their unusual upbringing can make them a little crazy. "It turns you into a real weirdo if you're a kid actor," he says. Nevertheless, he adds that "it's great training."

Joel D. Amos. "*Drive* Interview: Ryan Gosling Is in the Driver's Seat." Movie Fanatic, September 14, 2011. www.moviefanatic.com/2011/09/drive-interview-ryan-gosling-is-in-the-drivers-seat.

boom guy [that works the overhead microphone] had to throw down his mic and have a laugh attack in the corner."[38]

Carell admired Ryan's work in the pilot, as well, and found himself similarly awed by Ryan's comedy chops. "He's not known for his comedy, but he's hysterically funny," Carell says. "He's kind of a natural."[39] Despite the talent showcased in the pilot, however, the series was not picked up.

Breaking the Stigma

Following the disappointment around the failure of *The Unbelievables*, Ryan managed to land a part in the 2000 film *Remember the Titans*. Set in the early 1970s, the film is based on the true story of the newly desegregated T.C. Williams High School in Alexandria, Virginia, and the efforts of the school's black football coach, played by Denzel Washington, to integrate the racially divided football team. Ryan had a minor role in the film as one of the football players.

Gosling had a chance to work with movie star Denzel Washington in the movie Remember the Titans. *Gosling hoped a role in such a big picture would help launch his career as an adult actor.*

Although the film was a box office success, it received mixed reviews from the critics. Mick LaSalle, a film critic for the *San Francisco Chronicle*, praised the football scenes and noted that the film's theme of racial integration "is handled with sensitivity, and the characters, even those on the wrong side of history, are treated with humanity and respect."[40] Jeff Vice of the Salt Lake City, Utah, *Deseret News* wrote that the movie had "real heart and a worthwhile purpose for existing" and called it "surprisingly entertaining." Yet he also complained that the movie was "corny, clichéd and downright cheesy at times," as well as "predictable."[41] Meanwhile, Robert Wilonsky of the *Dallas Observer* noted, "Its heart is in the right place, but it has no soul. . . . This is indeed a true story, but it reads like the worst kind of fiction, one in which characters are made of tissue and dialogue is penned on placards."[42]

Despite being in a film with a Hollywood heavyweight such as the Academy Award–winning Washington, Ryan received little if any career advancement from his work in *Remember the Titans*. In part, this was because he only had a minor role. But it was also because, even though he was nearly out of his teens, he was still playing the part of a kid. He longed to be cast in a meatier, more adult role, but he had trouble shaking the image of himself as a child actor.

To make matters worse, because of his difficulties in landing adult roles, Ryan was dropped by his agent. "It's very hard coming from kids' television to break the stigma,"[43] he says. That stigma of having appeared on the *All New Mickey Mouse Club* and in *Young Hercules* meant that no director wanted to cast him in adult roles. As he approached his twentieth birthday, he began to feel like a failure and even considered giving up acting altogether. Ryan did not realize it, but his big break was right around the corner.

Chapter 3

Reinventing Ryan

While Ryan Gosling struggled to be taken seriously as an adult actor, he turned to independent films (indies) for the roles he was hungry to play—and found his first big break. Although he has appeared in a few big-budget studio films, he has preferred to stay with indies, where he can play a wide variety of characters. And—perhaps not surprisingly, given his musical roots—he has also returned to singing, which has continued to play a part in his career.

Breakout Role

After being dropped by his agent, Gosling was about to give up on his dream of becoming a performer. But then one day in 2000 he was helping a friend learn lines for an independent movie called *The Believer*. The movie was based on the true story of Danny Balint, a neo-Nazi who committed suicide after a report in the *New York Times* revealed that he was Jewish. Gosling was so impressed by the script that he contacted the director, Henry Bean, and begged for an audition. At first the director was reluctant to see him; after all, Gosling had never taken on such a weighty, dramatic role. But Gosling persisted, and Bean finally agreed to a meeting during his lunch hour. Ultimately, Bean offered Gosling the part of Balint, the lead role, because he believed that Gosling's own strict Mormon upbringing would help him relate to Balint's complex feelings about Judaism. The role would change Gosling's life.

Ryan Gosling played a Jewish neo-Nazi in the 2001 film The Believers. *The performance allowed Gosling to be considered for serious films.*

"I Would Act for Free"

The subject matter of *The Believer* was highly controversial. In fact, after a screening at the Simon Wiesenthal Center, a Jewish human-rights organization that was named after Nazi hunter Simon Wiesenthal, led to a protest against the film, no major distributor would touch the movie, and it had only a limited theatrical release. But that did not stop movie reviewers from raving about *The Believer*. Famed movie critic Roger Ebert called Gosling "a powerful young actor."[44] Peter Travers of *Rolling Stone* called the film "a fireball of contradictory ideas that will pin you to your seat" and noted, "Gosling gives a great, dare-anything performance that will be talked of for ages."[45]

The Believer turned out to be Gosling's breakout role. "I got the part and my life changed,"[46] he recalls. He was nominated for an Independent Spirit Award and a Chicago Film Critics Association Award for his performance, and he won a Russian Guild of Film Critics Award. The film itself won the Grand Jury Prize at the 2001 Sundance Film Festival. Gosling found the sudden rush of attention he was receiving a bit overwhelming. "Months earlier I was in New Zealand with a fake tan and leather pants, fighting imaginary sphinxes," he says. "After *The Believer* I was at Sundance, and people were talking to me about my craft."[47] It was, as the *New York Times* pointed out, "a drastic reinvention for a onetime child actor."[48]

Gosling was grateful that his work in the film helped him finally bridge the gap between child and adult roles. He says that *The Believer* "gift-wrapped for me the career that I have now."[49] But more than that, the movie helped him define what he wanted his career to be. He says that while working on this movie, "I realized I would act for free."[50] He felt like he had found his true calling and that he loved acting so much he would have done it regardless of how much it paid—or even whether it paid at all. After making *The Believer*, he came to an important realization: He wanted to continue working in independent films because of the freedom and creativity they afforded.

King of the Misfits

Gosling followed up the success of *The Believer* with a string of independent films that helped secure his place as a serious talent. The first of these was the 2002 psychological thriller *Murder by Numbers*, which costarred Sandra Bullock and Michael Pitt. Gosling and Pitt play a pair of high school misfits: smug, arrogant rich kids who plan and execute the murder of a random victim just to prove they can get away with it. Bullock plays a detective who investigates the case.

Although *Murder by Numbers* did well at the box office, it received mixed reviews. Mike Clark of *USA Today* complained that the movie often seemed "like two or three different movies" and was "plot-heavy and occasionally wobbly." But he praised Gosling and Pitt for their performances, saying that this "psychological drama is stolen by two standout supporting players."[51] Other reviewers also praised their performances, including independent reviewer Brian Rowe, who noted, "The scenes that truly sparkle with energy and vitality are the ones not with Sandra's character but with Pitt and Gosling." He described the two actors as "magnetic in their quiet, eerie scenes."[52] Roger Ebert added, "Many of the best scenes involve an intellectual and emotional duel between the two young men."[53]

After *Murder by Numbers*, Gosling played another misfit in *The Slaughter Rule* (2002). His character, Roy, a high school senior, gets cut from the school's football team soon after learning his estranged father has committed suicide. The movie focuses on the relationship between the emotionally troubled Roy and his equally disturbed football coach, played by veteran character actor David Morse. The film was nominated for the Grand Jury Prize at the 2002 Sundance Film Festival. Gosling's performance again attracted attention. The *New York Times* referred to him as "major star material" and said he possessed "a rawness and an intensity"[54] in the film.

Gosling played another dark character in *The United States of Leland* (2003). He played Leland P. Fitzgerald, a teenage boy who commits a murder. The movie did not do well at the box office and received mostly negative reviews. Nevertheless, it helped define Gosling as an actor with depth. In addition, although he played a high school student in each of the four independent films he had made up to this point, these movies all helped him make the transition into adult roles because the characters he was playing were darker and the plots of the films were more dramatic and serious.

"Everlasting Magic"

Gosling's next role was the one that launched his career into overdrive. Up until then, he had appeared in edgy indies that did not have the mass audience of a big studio film. But the 2004 film *The Notebook* brought Gosling to the attention of millions of viewers worldwide and turned him into a heartthrob.

Gosling's reputation as an actor had grown to the point that he no longer had to audition for roles. *The Notebook*'s director, Nick Cassavetes, told Gosling he wanted him for the role because he looked like an ordinary guy—just like the character.

The 2004 film The Notebook *was Gosling's first appearance in a major motion picture.*

"You're not handsome. You're not cool. . . . You're not a movie star," Cassavetes told him. "You're nuts. I could believe that you would meet a girl once and build a house for her."[55]

In the movie, which is based on the novel of the same title by Nicholas Sparks, Gosling plays a working-class young man named Noah in the early 1940s who falls in love with society

The Wrong Man for the Job

Susie Salmon is the narrator in Alice Sebold's 2002 book, *The Lovely Bones*, about a fourteen-year-old girl who is brutally raped and murdered. As she looks down from somewhere up above, Susie watches over her family and wants her murderer to be caught and brought to justice. Her father, Jack, is wild with grief over the heinous crime. Frustrated with the job investigators are doing, he sets out to catch the killer himself.

When cast members were chosen for the film version of *The Lovely Bones*, Ryan Gosling was given the role of Susie's father. Only twenty-six years old at the time, Gosling strongly believed that he was wrong for the part. "I just couldn't see myself as the father of this girl," he says. He called the director and said, "You must be nuts. I love the story, but me as the dad? You're crazy." But the director wanted Gosling for the part. In an effort to make himself look older, Gosling gained 60 pounds (27kg) and grew a full beard before production began. When he reported to the set, though, it soon became apparent that he was correct and was not the best fit for the role. That was when Mark Wahlberg, who is nine years older than Gosling, was chosen to take his place—a decision Gosling supported. "You have to know what you can't do," he says.

Quoted in Matt Mueller. "What Would His Mother Say?" *Guardian* (Manchester, UK), March 13, 2008. www.guardian.co.uk/film/2008/mar/14/1.

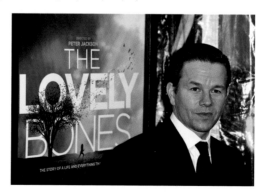

Mark Wahlberg at The Lovely Bones *premiere, New York, 2009.*

girl Allie, played by Rachel McAdams. Early in the movie, in order to get Allie to agree to go out with him, Noah dangles by one hand from a Ferris Wheel until she agrees to a date. This scene made the list of British magazine *Total Film*'s 50 Most Romantic Movie Moments of All Time. The movie itself landed on numerous lists of most romantic films, including *Us Weekly*'s 30 Most Romantic Movies of All Time.

Audiences were taken in by the story of star-crossed Allie and Noah, and *The Notebook* performed very well at the box office. A reviewer for the *Washington Post* wrote that Gosling was "particularly convincing as a young man who charms his way past a girl's strongest defenses."[56] Writing for the website Film Yap, Nick Rogers notes that "Gosling and McAdams spark something akin to cinematically everlasting magic."[57]

Despite the onscreen chemistry between Allie and Noah, in real life Gosling and McAdams did not get along on the set. There were frequent screaming matches between the two, and at one point during the filming, Gosling wanted the director to replace McAdams with a stand-in because he could not stand to look at her. Cassavetes said no. "It was a strange experience," Gosling says, "making a love story and not getting along with your co-star in any way."[58]

Somehow, the two young costars managed to translate the tension and anger between them into an award-winning onscreen passion. For his role as Noah, Gosling won numerous awards, including an MTV Movie Award and six Teen Choice Awards. Ironically, most of the awards he won, such as the MTV Movie Award for Best Kiss, were shared with McAdams.

A Huge Honor

After *The Notebook*, Gosling was suddenly seen as a successful mainstream Hollywood movie star. He could have followed up by taking on more leading-man roles in commercially successful studio films. But rather than cash in on the sudden attention, he chose to return to independent films. For his next role, he played a drug-addicted Brooklyn middle school teacher in *Half Nelson*. The seedy character of Dan Dunne, unkempt and hungover for most of the movie, was about as far removed from that of the handsome Noah as one could possibly imagine.

The movie was highly acclaimed. A reviewer for *LA Weekly* proclaimed that the movie was "so sobering and searingly truthful that watching it feels like being tossed from a calm beach into a raging current."[59] Reviews of Gosling's performance were equally glowing. One writer for *Entertainment Weekly* raved, "Without ever appearing to act, Gosling is the most exciting actor of his generation."[60]

Gosling received more than a dozen award nominations for his work in *Half Nelson*—including the most prestigious of all, the Academy Award for Best Actor. At only twenty-six years old, he became one of the youngest actors ever to be nominated for this award, an honor that surprised him. To him, his days in the Mickey Mouse Club did not seem that long ago. Gosling was also the first Canadian to be nominated for a Best Actor Oscar since Walter Pidgeon was nominated for the 1943 film *Madame Curie*. And although Gosling did not win the Oscar—the trophy went to Forest Whitaker for his performance as the demented Ugandan dictator Idi Amin in *The Last King of Scotland*—just being nominated for an Oscar was a huge accolade and career boost.

A Versatile Actor

By 2006 Gosling had established himself as a serious talent. He continued to prefer to work in independent films, and he has been particularly drawn to playing characters who are quirky or offbeat. He has also resisted being pigeonholed into any one type of character or genre and has demonstrated that he is adept at everything from thrillers to romantic comedy to drama.

In 2007 he played an up-and-coming lawyer in the thriller *Fracture*, in which he costarred with the Academy Award–winning Anthony Hopkins. Gosling said he was distracted by working opposite the legendary Hopkins and described their scenes together as "difficult because I'm such a fan of his that I'm always watching him and enjoying what he's doing. . . . He's a fascinating guy to watch."[61]

Reviewers generally agreed that he held his own against Hopkins in this courtroom drama. A reviewer for *LA Weekly* said, "He's the kind of actor who . . . can turn the way he slouches in a chair into a riveting bit of business."[62] For his performance in *Fracture*, Gosling was nominated for a Teen Choice Award.

Gosling's next role was probably his most offbeat thus far: the awkward and sweetly affected Lars in *Lars and the Real Girl*. Lars lives in a garage apartment and avoids physical contact and intimacy of any sort with other people. He falls in love with

*Ryan Gosling's performance as a quirky loner who loves a life-size blow-up doll in the 2007 film **Lars and the Real Girl** brought him new attention as a serious actor.*

a mail-order, life-size plastic doll named Bianca. The movie received mostly good reviews; the *Los Angeles Times* called it "the sweetest, most innocent, most completely enjoyable film around."[63] Gosling won a Satellite Award for Best Actor for his performance as Lars. Despite the accolades, however, the film had only a limited release and did not perform well at the box office. "When my films don't do well, I'm hurt and surprised," says Gosling. "It's discouraging."[64]

Dead Man's Bones

After completing his work on *Lars and the Real Girl*, Gosling decided to take a break from acting—a break that wound up lasting three years. During this time he decided to follow his long-

In a break from acting, Ryan Gosling and a friend started a band called Dead Man's Bones. Here Gosling plays with the Silverlake Conservatory Children's Choir in Los Angeles in 2010.

standing musical passion by forming a band with Zach Shields, a pal he met in 2005. The two of them have a mutual fascination with an odd assortment of things, including 1950s doo-wop bands, 1960s girl groups, ghosts and monsters, and the Haunted Mansion ride at Disneyland. So they decided to give their newly formed band a spooky-sounding name: Dead Man's Bones.

Neither Gosling nor Shields knew how to play an instrument—but they did not let that stop them. They spent a year learning to play their own instruments, including piano, guitar, drums, and bass. They also wrote all their own songs and played all the instruments for their album, which they recorded in bits and pieces over the course of several months. The album features the Silverlake Conservatory Children's Choir of Los Angeles on several of the songs, which have titles like "Flowers Grow Out of My Grave" and "Dead Hearts." But Gosling insists, "[The album] isn't as dark as it might seem, because to us it's a love story about monsters and ghosts and finding love."[65]

A video was released in 2008, and their self-titled debut album was released in 2009. That same year, they toured the United States and Canada. On each of their twelve tour stops, they performed with a local children's chorus, just as they had done when recording the album. Gosling and Shields were careful to explain everything to the kids and made sure they understood that the monsters and ghosts in the songs were meant to be funny and not scary.

In press photos for the band, Gosling is shown in costume as Frankenstein's monster and Shields is made up like a werewolf. This is in keeping with the spirit of the album, which Gosling describes as "spooky doo-wop."[66] A writer for the Boston Globe described its sound as "a soundtrack to a monster bash with [the 1960s girl group] the Shangri-Las as the house band."[67] One writer for LA Weekly praised Gosling's "deep, raspy voice" and exclaimed, "Not bad at all!"[68]

Stretching Himself Even Further

In 2010 Gosling returned to acting with a string of films that further demonstrated his acting versatility. He tackled another

For Help, Call the Gosline

When Ryan Gosling announced in March 2013 that he was taking a break from acting, he had no idea how this would crush his fans. Even after Gosling apologetically clarified that he was only taking a break to focus on directing and was not really going away, the Internet was alive with fans blogging, tweeting, commenting, and posting about how devastated they were at the idea of not being able to see their favorite hunk on the silver screen. Not long after Gosling's announcement, the British online movie and television streaming site Blinkbox sent out a tweet with an important message for distraught Ryan Gosling fans: They now had their very own twenty-four-hour helpline called the Gosline. Gosling fans could call the listed number and for a fee be soothed by Gosling's voice speaking his famous lines from *The Notebook*: "So it's not gonna be easy. It's gonna be really hard. We're gonna have to work at this every day, but I want to do that because I want you. I want all of you, forever, you and me, every day."

The Notebook. DVD. Directed by Nick Cassavetes. Los Angeles: New Line Cinema, 2004.

romantic drama with *Blue Valentine*, which depicts with gritty realism both the heady days at the beginning of a relationship and the disintegration of a marriage. The Charlottetown *Guardian* of Prince Edward Island, Canada, praised the film and said that Gosling and his costar, Michelle Williams, "bring an astoundingly authentic feel to their characters as they fall in and out of love."[69] Gosling was nominated for several awards for his performance and won the Chlotrudis Award for Best Actor from the Chlotrudis Society, a Boston-based organization that promotes independent filmmaking.

Gosling continued to flex his acting muscles in 2011 by appearing in three mainstream films. He won a Satellite Award for Best Actor for his portrayal of a stuntman in the thriller

Drive—in which he has almost no dialogue. One interviewer commented, "What's most daring about *Drive* is not the violence, but Gosling's ability to sustain tension without saying a word."[70]

Gosling switched gears again by playing a womanizer in his first romantic comedy, *Crazy, Stupid, Love*, along with his old pal Steve Carell. He had wanted to do a comedy ever since he and Carell had worked on the failed pilot for *The Unbelievables*. Gosling proved to audiences that he could be funny on film, particularly in one scene in which he slaps Carell in the face right in the middle of a conversation. His performance in *Crazy, Stupid, Love* earned him a Golden Globe nomination.

He was also nominated for a Golden Globe for the political drama *The Ides of March*, in which he played a campaign manager. In this film, Gosling stretched himself yet again by taking on something that was unfamiliar to him. "I'm Canadian and so American politics aren't really in my wheelhouse [that is, part of his personal experience],"[71] he explains. He took the role as a way to become more politically aware; but there was another benefit involved for him—the chance to work with actor George Clooney. Clooney not only costarred in the movie, he also directed it and cowrote the screenplay. After watching Clooney work, Gosling became inspired to become a director himself one day.

A Big Announcement

Gosling had appeared in so many films that by late 2011 he began to worry about overexposure. He wondered whether he was making too many movies and commented, "It would be nice to have time in between [movies] for people to forget one character and accept another."[72] It was not long before he decided to do just that. In March 2013 he announced that he was taking a break from acting to reevaluate his career. "I need a break from myself as much as I imagine the audience does,"[73] he explained. There was such an outcry from his fans, however, that a few days later he made another statement to clarify his intent. At the premiere of his most current film, *The Place Beyond the Pines*, Gosling apologized to his fans, clarifying that he was just taking a break from acting so he could focus on directing.

In fact, Gosling was already in the middle of directing his first movie when he made that big announcement, a fantasy film titled *How to Catch a Monster*. Gosling not only directed it but

Actress Christina Hendricks (left) stars in How to Catch a Monster, *Gosling's 2014 directorial debut.*

wrote the screenplay as well. Marc Platt, the producer, praised Gosling for his "beautifully haunting script."[74] The movie stars *Mad Men* star Christina Hendricks as a single mom whose son stumbles upon a mysterious underwater village. It was filmed in Detroit, Michigan, in the spring of 2013 and scheduled for release in 2014.

Gosling has also expanded his horizons by serving as a producer for four films, beginning with *Blue Valentine*. He was also a producer of the 2010 documentary *ReGeneration*, which he also narrated, and of the 2013 crime thriller *Only God Forgives*, in which he also stars. Finally, he produced his film *How to Catch a Monster*.

Always one to challenge himself by taking on varied and complex acting roles, Gosling sees his foray into directing and producing as an extension of that same creative drive. "You can't act forever," he says. "You have a shelf life as an actor, so you have to find another way to express yourself."[75] Whether acting, producing, or directing, it seems that Gosling is going to be involved in filmmaking for some time to come.

Chapter 4

At Home with Ryan

Although Ryan Gosling has made it big in Hollywood, he is still very much the same humble, hardworking guy from Canada who loves his mother and sister—and his dog—very much. He keeps very busy in his personal life and pursues a wide variety of interests, both as pastimes and in a more serious vein. Although his romantic life has often been the subject of tabloid headlines, Gosling has managed to avoid many of the pitfalls that have derailed many others in Hollywood.

Man's Best Friend

When Gosling first moved to Los Angeles in 1999, he chose to live near the downtown area, rather than in Hollywood or Beverly Hills, where many movie stars typically live. He bought a house there and was soon joined by George, an orange mixed-breed dog who is Gosling's constant companion and often accompanies him to movie sets. Gosling once referred to George as "the great love of my life."[76] In fact, George made an appearance with Gosling on *Late Night with Jimmy Fallon* in 2011, during which Gosling showed his affection for his dog by biting off pieces of apple for George to eat.

Shortly after turning thirty years old in 2010, Gosling decided to take George and move to New York City after living in Los Angeles for more than a decade. He wanted to relocate in order to gain new experience. "It's hard to play a real person when you've been [pampered] in jets and town cars," he says. "In Los Angeles, it's easy to lose touch with everything. You just sit in your car the whole time. In New York, you're forced to deal with life, it's there in front of you on a daily basis."[77]

Relaxing with Ryan

Gosling has very little free time, but when he is not working, he enjoys spending time at home doing a variety of things—especially playing with George. An avid animal lover, Gosling likes to spend time horseback riding, too. And for years he has loved riding motorcycles and owns a dirt bike, which he often rides for fun. Other favorite pastimes include reading and playing music; he is particularly fond of playing jazz guitar and piano. Along with playing music, he loves to listen to music, as well, and his iPod contains plenty of tunes by ambient master Brian Eno, 1950s jazz trumpeter and vocalist Chet Baker, and the electronic alternative duo

Ryan Gosling's dog, George, is Gosling's constant companion. Here George joins Gosling on Late Night with Jimmy Fallon.

Glass Candy. He also enjoys making furniture, which he learned how to do for his role in *The Notebook*.

Gosling likes to be active, and he tries to work out once a week. Ballet is another physical activity of his; he took lessons as a child and continues to study ballet at a studio whenever he can. Most of his classmates, he says, are little girls, who seem amused by his presence and try to offer him encouragement. "They try and be positive but I'm so bad," he says. "I don't even know what I like about it but it's like acting, I'm just compelled to do it."[78]

Gosling seems to delight in indulging his inner child, as well. When in California, he loves to visit the Magic Castle in Hollywood. This is a private nightclub and restaurant in a castle-like building complete with turrets. It is a favorite hangout for magicians and magic lovers, and it often features magic shows and other variety acts.

Of course, among Gosling's all-time favorite places to visit are Disney World and Disneyland. In fact, he still goes to Disneyland whenever he is in the Los Angeles area. "It still kind of resonates with me,"[79] he explains. He frequently goes there alone, disguised by a hat and large sunglasses. Among his favorite attractions there are the Haunted Mansion and the Enchanted Tiki Room.

Even though he often goes to public places where there are a lot of people, Gosling says he really does not get recognized very often. "You just have to hang out in places that are more interesting than you are,"[80] he quips. When he does get recognized, oftentimes it is because someone has mistaken him for another famous Ryan. Some fans confuse Gosling with Ryan Reynolds, who is also Canadian. People frequently approach him for an autograph and then are disappointed to learn he is a different Ryan than they thought.

"A Constant Inspiration"

Of all the places he visits, Gosling's favorite will always be his mother's house. He spends as many holidays as he can with his mother back in Burlington, Ontario, and remains very close to

Gosling, Ink

One look at Ryan Gosling's many tattoos and it becomes obvious that he is a man with eclectic interests. Gracing his left shoulder is a tattoo from the cover of the popular children's book *The Giving Tree*, which his mother used to read to him and his sister. Another tattoo, this one on Gosling's inside left bicep, is a ghostly likeness of Theda Bara, an American actress who starred in silent films and in stage productions between 1914 and 1926. Tattooed across Gosling's inner left wrist is a solid black band, and on his upper left forearm are the initials "W.H.R." (Gosling has not made public the meaning of these initials.)

One of Gosling's tattoos did not turn out quite the way he had planned. He intended to create the image of a monster's hand dropping a bloody heart. But when he used a do-it-yourself kit to do his own inking, the tattoo bore no resemblance to his original idea. "A lot of people think it's a cactus," says Gosling. "It's become a bit of an ink blot [on a Rorschach test]: you see what you want to."

Quoted in Catherine Shoard. "Ryan Gosling: Life in the Fast Lane." *Guardian* (Manchester, UK), September 23, 2011. www.guardian.co.uk/film/2011/sep/24/ryan-gosling-drive-crazy-stupid.

Gosling has several tattoos, including one that he did on himself.

his sister, Mandi, as well. He often takes one or both of them with him to events, such as in 2013 when he took Donna as his date to the world premiere of *Gangster Squad* in Los Angeles. In 2007 both Donna and Mandi accompanied him to the Academy Awards ceremony when he was nominated for *Half Nelson*. Gosling demonstrated his deep affection for his mom during the ceremony; she had chosen to wear her hair in a beehive because she thought the hairstyle would be all the rage at the Oscars that night, but she was embarrassed because no one else was wearing their hair that way. Even more embarrassing for Donna was that the person seated directly behind her in the theater, actress Rachel Weisz, had to crane to see around Donna's big hairdo.

Because Gosling was nominated for the Best Actor Oscar, he and his mother and sister were sitting in the center of the front row, which only added to Donna's self-consciousness. Gosling noticed that his mother was sinking down in her seat, too mortified to enjoy the big evening. So he did what any good son would do: He turned to the person seated next to him, acclaimed actress Meryl Streep, and quietly told her what was happening, asking her to help. Streep graciously obliged; at the next commercial break, she leaned over and said to Donna that she had almost worn her hair in a beehive, too, and was jealous of Donna's coif. Thanks to her son's intervention and Streep's cooperation, Donna glowed for the rest of the evening.

Gosling is immensely proud of his mother. When she graduated from college in 2011 and became a high school teacher, he beamed, "My mom is a constant inspiration to me. . . . She gave me the self-confidence to try and have the life that I want, to try and live my dreams."[81] Gosling shows his appreciation for his mother's hard work of raising two kids as a single parent by sending her a card for both Mother's and Father's Day. Perhaps because of the good relationship he enjoys with his mom, Gosling looks forward to becoming a father himself someday. His paternal instinct showed itself during the filming of *The Place Beyond the Pines*, in which he played the father of an infant. Gosling bonded with the baby on the set and even spent time cradling and feeding his little costar.

For her part, Donna is fiercely proud of her son, not only because of his professional accomplishments but also because of the kind of person he is. "I was able to teach him how to use a razor," she says. "But he's had to teach himself to be a man. It's something he's always taken so seriously."[82]

Costar Chemistry

Gosling's personal life is very rich and rewarding—and his romantic life has been no exception. Over the years, he has had a habit of dating his costars. He describes working together as

Despite their early and well-documented dislike of one another while filming The Notebook, *Ryan Gosling and actress Rachel McAdams (right) began dating in 2005. The relationship ended in 2008.*

"the best way to get to know someone," and he finds this is especially true when it comes to making movies. "When you work creatively with somebody, it's very telling and you sort of fast-track with everyone."[83]

Gosling has had several high-profile romances. While filming *Murder by Numbers*, Gosling and costar Sandra Bullock both felt their onscreen chemistry turn into something more. Although there was a substantial age difference between them—he was twenty-one and she was thirty-seven—the two began a real-life romance in early 2002. But finding time to be together proved difficult, with both their careers in full swing. There were frequent separations while one or both of them filmed on location. After more than a year of dating, the strain of trying to

Ryan Gosling began dating costar Eva Mendes (right) during the filming of **The Place Beyond the Pines.**

carry on a long-distance relationship took its toll, and they split up in July 2003.

The sixteen-year age difference between Gosling and Bullock raised some eyebrows, but his next relationship really floored people. Two years after completing work on *The Notebook*, Gosling ran into Rachel McAdams in New York City. As the two of them talked, they both began to reconsider their previous opinions of one another. It was not long before sparks began to fly between them again—but this time they were sparks of another sort. The two began dating in June 2005, and no one was more puzzled by their relationship than Nick Cassavetes, the director of *The Notebook*. "They hated each other," he said. "And now they're dating?"[84]

Gosling and McAdams shared much in common—beginning with their hometown. McAdams is also Canadian, and in fact was born in London, Ontario, in the very same hospital as Gosling. There was also less of an age difference between the pair; McAdams is only two years older than Gosling. Perhaps one of the most important things in their favor is the fact that Gosling's mother and McAdams developed a deep bond. "His mom loved her,"[85] one of Gosling's friends explains.

Their relationship had its ups and downs, however. After dating for two years, they broke up, then reconciled a year later. But the reconciliation was short-lived, and by November 2008 they had split for good. Gosling has fond memories of their time together, and he has never spoken unkindly about any of his exes in public. In fact, he once referred to Sandra Bullock and Rachel McAdams as "two of the greatest girlfriends of all time."[86]

After splitting with McAdams, Gosling dated several other actresses briefly, including Kat Dennings in late 2009, Blake Lively in late 2010, and Olivia Wilde in early 2011. Later in 2011 he found himself again beginning a relationship when romance bloomed between him and costar Eva Mendes during the filming of *The Place Beyond the Pines* in upstate New York. The two found they had several things in common, including a love of dogs (of course, Gosling had George with him on the set). Their relationship grew as they spent more and more time together. After filming wrapped, Gosling and Mendes headed to one of his favorite places: Disneyland. The two next traveled to Paris to spend Thanksgiving together. By New Year's Day 2012, Gosling was introducing Mendes to his mother.

Gosling and Mendes have been in a steady relationship since September 2011. "Ryan is obsessed—he wants to see Eva all the time,"[87] a friend of Gosling's commented to an interviewer. His mother, who was disappointed by her son's breakup with McAdams, has nonetheless warmed to his new girlfriend. When Donna accompanied her son to the premiere of *Gangster Squad* in early 2013, she even wore an outfit culled from Mendes's closet.

Dealing with Stardom

Gosling is frequently in the company of many high-profile movie stars, yet he has managed—for the most part—to avoid the pitfalls of stardom. Many young actors, male and female alike, have fallen prey to the problems that can plague Hollywood stars, such as chronic alcohol and drug abuse. After the success of *The Notebook*, Gosling suddenly found himself the object of adoration by female fans. That kind of recognition and attention can be overwhelming, especially when it happens all of a sudden and the person is very young; Gosling was only twenty-three. He thinks the reason so many stars turn to substance abuse after becoming successful is that they have lots of money and too much free time, which translates into boredom and a lack of purpose. So Gosling found a constructive, healthy, and unique way to deal with the stress of becoming an overnight megastar: He took a job making sandwiches at a deli in Hollywood. "I'd never had a real job," he explains. Once he started working at the deli, people began to request that Gosling make their sandwiches. But he attributes that fact to something other than his fame. "I put love in those sandwiches!"[88] he says.

Gosling has had a brush with the law, however. On March 17, 2005, he was arrested in Los Angeles. Police officers charged him with driving under the influence of alcohol and/or drugs. Rather than pleading guilty to the original charge, Gosling accepted a plea bargain. His lawyers were able to negotiate a lesser charge known as "exhibiting speed," to which Gosling pleaded no contest. He received two years' probation and was ordered by the court to pay $849 in fines.

One of the Good Guys

That incident was not made public for years, and when Gosling fans hear about it now, they are often surprised because such escapades are uncharacteristic of Gosling. In fact, Gosling is more often in the news for helping *others* who are in trouble, rather than for being in trouble himself.

In his new hometown of New York City, Ryan Gosling has been known to intervene in altercations on the street.

For example, in August 2011 in New York City, Gosling had just finished working out at a gym and was walking along a street in Manhattan when he saw that a fight had broken out between two men. He dropped the bag he was carrying, walked over to step between them, and stopped any more punches from being thrown. Gosling learned that one of the men was an artist and the other a fan who could not afford to buy the artist's paintings—so he had stolen one.

Nearly seven months later, in early April 2012, Gosling again intervened in a New York City incident—and this time he saved a woman's life. British journalist Laurie Penny was about to cross Sixth Avenue and did not see that a speeding taxicab was bearing down on her. Gosling saw this happening and screamed to her to watch out as he pulled her out of the way. Penny did not realize who he was until a woman standing next to her remarked about how lucky she was to have been saved by Ryan Gosling. Penny then took to Twitter to let her forty thousand followers know who had saved her. "I literally, LITERALLY just got saved from a car by Ryan Gosling,"[89] Penny tweeted.

A Taste of Morocco

It is not only on the streets of New York City that the public has bumped elbows with Gosling. He is co-owner of a restaurant in Beverly Hills and often appears there. One of his more delectable ventures, the restaurant evolved from a spur-of-the-moment decision. He got a phone call in the early 2000s from his longtime friend Chris Angulo, who suggested that they go in together and buy a Beverly Hills restaurant called Mamounia. At the time, that sort of investment was the furthest thing from Gosling's mind. "I never really wanted to own it," he says. During his conversation with Angulo, Gosling learned that the current owner (Angulo's cousin) was leaving town and needed to sell the restaurant. Angulo wanted to buy it and convert it into a Moroccan restaurant, and he said the decision needed to be made immediately—meaning that same night. Gosling, who was already a huge fan of Moroccan food, decided to go for it.

Food "Made with Love"

While Abdessamad ("Chef Ben") Benameur was growing up in his home country of Morocco, he learned to cook at a young age by watching his mother. She shopped for food at the local markets, bought whatever was fresh that day, and then lovingly prepared meals for her family. These are Benameur's memories, and they fueled his passion for food and cooking. When he left Morocco and came to the United States, Benameur began using his mother's recipes to cater special events in the Los Angeles area. A rising star named Ryan Gosling tasted Benameur's cuisine and became an instant fan, later remarking that it was food he would eat every day for the rest of his life.

Before long Gosling and Benameur became good friends. They also became business partners, opening a restaurant in Beverly Hills called Tagine, where Benameur is head chef. He is proud to follow in his mother's footsteps, and like her, he uses only the freshest local ingredients for all the dishes he creates. It is also Benameur's wish for everyone who dines at Tagine to feel at home there. "All I want," he says, "is a warm place where the food is made with love."

Quoted in Tagine Beverly Hills. www.taginebeverlyhills.com.

"At the time, I wasn't very busy," he says, "so I spent all my money on this restaurant."[90]

Gosling and Angulo became the new owners along with a third partner, Abdessamad Benameur, a respected chef from Morocco who is known as Chef Ben. Together they chose a name for their restaurant: Tagine (pronounced *Tah-ZHEEN*). The word has a double meaning, referring to the earthenware pots that are used for traditional Moroccan cooking, as well as the spicy lamb or fish and vegetable stews that are cooked in the pots.

When Gosling said he had spent all his money to buy the restaurant, he was not kidding. At the time he was still an up-and-coming actor, and his financial status reflected that. So, when extensive (and expensive) renovations were needed before the restaurant could open, he had no choice but to do much of the work himself. For approximately a year he worked on the building, including six months spent installing new plumbing. When the work was finished and Tagine was finally ready to open, Gosling knew that all his hard work had finally paid off. "Now I love it," he says. "I think it's one of the best restaurants in L.A."[91]

Although Gosling's schedule is packed and he spends a great deal of time on location filming movies, he stays as involved as possible with Tagine's operation, including helping to choose the menu. In the years since the restaurant opened, he has helped out in the kitchen, waited tables, and even washed dishes, as well as helped Benameur with his Moroccan cooking classes. "I find it very special," says Benameur. "He's always involved."[92]

Whether hanging out with George, hitting the gym, visiting with his loved ones, or indulging his taste for Moroccan cuisine, Gosling stays busy, and as he nears his mid-thirties, he is very happy with his rich and rewarding personal life. Even with these varied interests and a busy filmmaking schedule, Gosling still finds time to support the causes he feels strongly about.

Chapter 5

Ryan's Causes

Ryan Gosling is very active in his support of several social causes that are close to his heart. He has been involved in numerous humanitarian efforts from Mississippi to Africa. In addition, he is a supporter of women's rights and has spoken out against sexism in the movie industry. He has also spoken out publicly in support of the humane treatment of animals. One interviewer said that he found in Gosling "nothing egotistical or pretentious, just a very straight forward man who is trying to make the world a better place."[93]

Refugees in Chad

Gosling has been involved in several humanitarian efforts in various regions in Africa. From 2003 to 2010 civil war raged in the Darfur region of Sudan. The lengthy and violent conflict has spawned numerous humanitarian crises, including the displacement of more than 2.8 million people. Hundreds of thousands of Sudanese refugees, many of them wounded, fled across the border into nearby Chad, where they sought refuge in camps that have barely been able to meet so many people's basic need for food, water, shelter, and medical care. In January 2005 Gosling visited some of these refugee camps as part of the documentary *A Place in Time*. Directed by actress Angelina Jolie, the documentary features the camera work of numerous celebrities who videotaped the daily life of people in twenty-seven different locations around the world all at the same moment.

The first camp Gosling visited held thousands of children. Many of these children had been separated from their parents

Ryan Gosling arrived at the 2005 MTV Movie Awards wearing this T-shirt to raise awareness of the thousands of refugees from Darfur.

or orphaned; some had been attacked and physically injured or even raped by soldiers. "I had been briefed on what they had probably been through, a list of things. I tried to prepare myself for that. I wanted to be respectful, and I didn't want to be too prying," Gosling recalls. "I ended up being surrounded by something like a hundred kids, who were all looking up at me. . . . It was really quiet. They were all just following me and watching me."[94]

Gosling was reluctant to interview the children about their experiences because he did not want to stir up any traumatic memories of the violence and loss they had suffered. He describes what he did instead:

> We made little films together. I gave them the camera, and they filmed each other. They were just really cool. One kid made sunglasses out of a piece of unexposed negative film, and so when he looked through the glasses, he could see pictures. Another kid made a hat out of vodka bottle labels. They were just really creative, and cool. And I liked them. And so, when I left, they weren't just these faceless kids anymore. There was a small group of them that I felt I got to know. And so I felt invested in them after that experience.[95]

Gosling was deeply moved by the plight of the refugees he visited. He says, "I think with anybody who goes to Africa, the experience never leaves, certainly the kids don't."[96] In 2008 he spoke at Campus Progress's National Conference, where he helped raised awareness about the situation in the Darfur region and the plight of the refugees he had visited.

"A Trail of Human Destruction"

While he was in Chad, Gosling learned of another travesty in Africa that spurred him to action. He began hearing stories of thousands of children in the nearby country of Uganda who had been abducted and forced to become child soldiers or sex slaves. He traveled to Uganda in February 2007 with John Prendergast of the Enough Project, a humanitarian group that works to end crimes against humanity. While there, Gosling was horrified by what he learned about the violence against Ugandan children. "It's gruesome," he says. "You can't believe it."[97]

Gosling was so moved by the situation that he cowrote a movie script with his friend Noaz Deshe called *The Lord's Resistance Army*, about the child soldiers in Uganda. Unfortunately he has faced a lot of resistance in Hollywood to making the movie, particularly in getting funding for the project. "A movie with children and violence that's *true* is very difficult to get made,"[98] he explains, as most people do not want to know about such ugliness let alone pay to see it. Every backer he has approached has wanted to use big-name celebrities in the film to raise its profile and attract viewers, but Gosling has refused, wanting instead to feature the African children who have experienced these horrors firsthand. Although he has yet to make the movie, Gosling continues to work on behalf of the child soldiers. He is a supporter of Invisible Children, an organization that works to raise awareness about the Lord's Resistance Army. This army, which operates in several countries in Africa, including Uganda and Sudan, is accused of several human rights violations, including murder, kidnapping, mutilation, and forcing children to become sex slaves or child soldiers.

In 2010 Gosling returned to Africa with Prendergast, this time to visit eastern Congo. There, war has raged over control of so-called conflict minerals—minerals that are needed to make electronic devices such as mobile phones, computers, and MP3 players. The sites from which these minerals are mined are often in remote areas, and workers face many dangers and human rights abuses there, such as working long hours under very dangerous conditions for little or no pay. The majority of these sites are policed by armed rebel groups that force people, including children, to work in the mines for up to forty-eight hours at a stretch. Mudslides and cave-ins frequently threaten the miners' safety. In addition, the rebel groups commonly subject the miners and nearby residents to rape and other forms of violence in order to control them. Many villages have been looted or burned down and their residents slaughtered by these rebel groups, and fighting over control of the industry has led to widespread, ongoing armed conflict.

The Enough Project

Conceived in 2006 by a small group of activists and policy makers, the Enough Project is committed to ending genocide and crimes against humanity around the world. The group's mission is to help people from all walks of life understand the steps they can take to help make a difference in the world and put an end to these heinous actions—actions that are far more common than most people realize. Enough Project members conduct field research in countries that are plagued by genocide and crimes against humanity, develop policies to address these crises, and share tools to help empower citizens and groups working to enact change.

Ryan Gosling is one of several famous individuals who are devoted to the work of the Enough Project. Cofounder John Prendergast thinks that celebrities who use their fame to build awareness about some of the world's most vulnerable people are making an important difference. "They have educated countless people and shined a light on issues that would otherwise remain shrouded in darkness," says Prendergast. "By recruiting thousands of people to relatively unknown causes, they help create a real pressure for change."

Quoted in Jonathan Hutson. "How Celebrities Are Making a Difference for Human Rights: The Enough Project Launches Celebrity Upstanders Database." Enough Project, July 28, 2011. www.enoughproject.org/news/how-celebrities-are-making-difference-human-rights-enough-project-launches-celebrity-upstanders.

While in Congo Gosling made a video for the Enough Project called *Raise Hope for Congo* to help spread awareness of the situation there. He shot original footage for the video, which consists of short portraits of people who have been affected by violence in the region. Gosling and Prendergast cowrote an article for the *Huffington Post* in which they stated that Congo was in the midst of a "war which most people

Miners dig for tin ore in Congo. The mineral is used in computers and mobile phones. Hundreds of boys and young men work here in dangerous conditions for small salaries. In 2010 Gosling made a video about some of the workers in the mines.

know nothing about, despite the fact that we're all directly connected to it. Armed groups are fighting over the lucrative minerals that power our cell phones and laptops, leaving a trail of human destruction."[99]

Volunteering Closer to Home

In 2005 Gosling took part in a humanitarian effort that was closer to home. In August of that year, Hurricane Katrina, one of the deadliest and most destructive hurricanes to strike the United States, took the lives of more than eighteen hundred people and destroyed countless homes and buildings when it raged through Florida, Louisiana, Mississippi, Alabama, and other parts of the southeastern United States. Those who escaped with their lives lost property, belongings, pets, and other valuables they were forced to leave behind. Because of the devastation caused by Katrina, Gosling decided to lend a hand. He packed up a car and drove to Biloxi, Mississippi, which had been especially hard-hit by the hurricane. There he worked alongside other volunteers to help rebuild a monastery. Even after his initial visit to Mississippi, Gosling returned to the state several times, to continue helping out.

Gosling supports other causes as well. He is involved in the Canadian charity SickKids Foundation, which works to help

A fallen street sign is indicative of the ruin that befell Biloxi, Mississippi, after Hurricane Katrina in 2005. Gosling volunteered to help Katrina victims in the city.

children in Canada and around the world by funding research into children's health issues. He also supports the Silverlake Conservatory of Music, which provides low-cost or free music lessons and instruments to kids in the Los Angeles area.

"No Excuse"

Besides supporting several charities that aid children, Gosling has also been involved in many charities that work for animal rights. A lifelong animal lover, Gosling has spoken out against animal cruelty a number of times. He has campaigned to encourage the KFC and McDonald's restaurant chains to improve the way they treat chickens. For example when Gosling learned that such chickens are raised in dark and extremely cramped quarters and often suffer broken bones from rough handling, he decided to take action. So he teamed up with the animal rights group People for the Ethical Treatment of Animals (PETA) in 2003 to write a letter to the KFC restaurants in Canada. The letter urged the restaurants to raise their chickens more humanely. He wrote the company again in 2008 to complain about horrific conditions in poultry slaughterhouses. In 2010 he wrote a similar letter to McDonald's on PETA's behalf to urge the company to stop scalding chickens to death and opt for a less cruel method of slaughter. Despite much public outcry, chicken suppliers for these restaurant chains still use this method for slaughtering chickens.

Gosling continued his campaign on behalf of these birds when he learned of a method used to kill chickens and turkeys that have been exposed to disease. The method, which is endorsed by the U.S. Department of Agriculture (USDA), exterminates the birds by submerging them in firefighting foam, which slowly suffocates them. The process can take up to fifteen minutes, and opponents of it claim it causes the birds prolonged suffering and trauma. In 2011 Gosling decided to speak out against this practice by again teaming up with PETA. He wrote a letter on behalf of the animal rights group to the USDA, asking the agency to revoke its approval of this method. Gosling pointed out that "if dogs and cats were

No Child Should Be Invisible

Founded in 2004, the group called Invisible Children works to raise worldwide awareness of Uganda's brutal guerilla leader, Joseph Kony. Leading the most-wanted list of the International Criminal Court, Kony's rebel group, which is known as the Lord's Resistance Army (LRA), has committed untold numbers of atrocities. The LRA has kidnapped thousands of children, turning the boys into child soldiers and the girls into sex slaves. The Invisible Children website states: "We first encountered these atrocities in northern Uganda in 2003 when we met a boy named Jacob who feared for his life and a woman named Jolly who had a vision for a better future. Together, we promised Jacob that we would do whatever we could to stop Joseph Kony and the LRA."

To raise awareness and inspire global action, Invisible Children uses a number of techniques, such as creating documentary films. One film, which was released in March 2012, was titled simply *Kony 2012* and in a very short time received massive worldwide attention. Numerous celebrities began sending out tweets to implore their followers to watch the film and support Invisible Children, including Ryan Gos-

ling, Rihanna, Justin Bieber, and Oprah Winfrey. Within six days the film had reached 100 million views on YouTube, and worldwide awareness of the LRA's atrocities soared.

Invisible Children. "About: Invisible Children Exists to Bring a Permanent End to LRA Atrocities." http://invisiblechildren.com/about.

To help raise awareness of the film Kony 2012, released by the group Invisible Children, Gosling tweeted his fans to see the film and tell others about it.

killed in this way, the person committing these acts would be charged with cruelty to animals."[100] Gosling urged the USDA to endorse a more humane method to euthanize sick birds that has been approved by veterinarians. As of 2013, however, the USDA still had not revoked its approval of using the foam to euthanize diseased poultry.

Pigs, too, have a place in Gosling's heart. In 2012 Gosling joined several other celebrities in protesting the treatment of pigs by Walmart after an undercover investigation exposed horrific cruelty at one of the farms that supplies pork to the retail giant. On behalf of the animal protection organization Mercy for Animals, Gosling, along with Zooey Deschanel, Emily Deschanel, Tom Morello, Kim Basinger, David Boreanaz, Ed Begley Jr., John Francis Daley, James Cromwell, Steve-O, and Loretta Swit, penned a letter to Walmart's chief operating officer, Mike Duke. The letter implored Duke to help put a stop to the "needless suffering of these animals" by no longer buying pork from suppliers that "confine pigs in cages so small they can't even turn around for nearly their entire lives."[101] Protests against Walmart's treatment of pigs continued in 2013.

Gosling has also spoken out against inhumane practices in the cattle industry. He was upset to discover that dairy farmers routinely practice a process called dehorning, in which calves' sensitive horn tissue is burned away with hot irons or chemicals, gouged out with sharp metal instruments, or hewn off with handsaws. This process is done to prevent the cattle from injuring each other, themselves, or people and is often performed without any anesthesia. Animal rights activists claim the process causes intense pain, fear, and suffering for the young calves. In 2013 Gosling again partnered with PETA and wrote a letter to Jerry Kozak, the president and chief executive officer of the National Milk Producers Federation. In it, Gosling urged Kozak to require farmers to stop dehorning and instead use selective breeding to produce naturally hornless cattle. In the letter, Gosling insisted there was "absolutely no reason—and no excuse—for the cruel, unnecessary practice of dehorning to continue."[102]

Protesting Sexism in the Film Industry

In addition to his concern for animals and children, Gosling is also a supporter of women's rights, something that stems from his close relationship with his mother and sister. "I feel like I think like a woman, because I grew up with my mother and my sister so I've just been programmed to think like a girl,"[103] he says. "I wouldn't know how to think any other way."[104]

Gosling's empathy for women became apparent during the controversy over the rating for his film *Blue Valentine*. The movie initially received a rating of NC-17 from the Motion

Ryan Gosling protested the NC-17 rating that his 2010 film Blue Valentine *received, believing that the rating was indicative of sexism in the industry.*

"If there's any justice, Ryan Gosling and Michelle Williams will both earn Oscar nominations for their raw, arresting performances."
ENTERTAINMENT WEEKLY, Dan Krager

RYAN GOSLING   MICHELLE WILLIAMS

BLUE VALENTINE

A LOVE STORY

Picture Association of America (MPAA), which rates films according to their content. An NC-17 rating is the strictest one employed. Whereas an R rating would allow children under age seventeen to be admitted into a theater with a parent or legal guardian, a rating of NC-17 means no one under seventeen can be admitted. The MPAA gave *Blue Valentine* the NC-17 rating because of an extremely intense, but non-nude, sex scene.

The rating seemed unfair to Gosling. "I was very confused. It seems like I don't really understand this rating system," he comments, adding, "It seemed like there are horror movies that are like torture-porn that are R rated."[105] Gosling felt that the MPAA was using an inconsistent standard in its rating, as he points out: "How is it possible that these movies that torture women in a sexual context can have an R rating but a husband and wife making love is inappropriate?"[106]

Gosling released a statement in which he accused the MPAA of sexism. "It's misogynistic [women-hating] in nature to try and control a woman's sexual presentation of self. I consider this an issue that is bigger than this film."[107] Furthermore, because an NC-17 rating would mean that the movie could not be shown in major theater chains or even advertised on TV, which would seriously affects its profits, the director and the distributor of the movie challenged the rating. The MPAA eventually gave in and awarded the film the less restrictive R rating.

On the lighter side, Gosling's support of women has earned him the attention of feminist blogger Danielle Henderson. A graduate student in gender studies, Henderson created a blog called *The Feminist Ryan Gosling,* in which she posted photos of Gosling paired with witty feminist captions. The blog became so popular among fans that it spawned a book by the same name.

Gosling has shown himself to be a sensitive, compassionate, and caring young man with a social conscience. He is not afraid to speak out against what he sees as cruel or unfair conditions, and he often takes action when he sees an injustice. In today's world of often self-obsessed celebrities, he shines as an example of a person trying to do the right thing. His selfless attitude and his talent make it likely that he will be in the news for years to come.

Introduction: The Secret to His Success

1. Quoted in Michelle Tauber. "The Chemistry of Ryan Gosling." *People*, January 21, 2013, p. 66.
2. Dennis Lim. "A Heartthrob Finds His Tough-Guy Side." *New York Times*, September 14, 2011. www.nytimes.com /2011/09/18/movies/ryan-gosling-and-ides-of-march.html ?pagewanted=all&_r=0.
3. Jake Coyle. "Gosling at Ease in Every Role Except Movie Star." Associated Press, March 20, 2013. http://bigstory.ap .org/article/gosling-ease-every-role-except-movie-star.
4. Quoted in Matt Mueller. "What Would His Mother Say?" *Guardian* (Manchester, UK), March 13, 2008. www.guardian .co.uk/film/2008/mar/14/1.
5. *Guardian* (Charlottetown, Prince Edward Island, Canada). "Ryan Gosling Says Onscreen Intimacy in *Blue Valentine* 'Just Happened,'" January 24, 2011. www.theguardian.pe .ca/Canada---World/Arts/2011-01-04/article-2089490/Ryan -Gosling-says-onscreen-intimacy-in-Blue-Valentine-just -happened/1.
6. Quoted in NPR. "Ryan Gosling: Fully Immersed in 'Blue Valentine.'" Transcript, December 15, 2010. www.wbur .org/npr/131963261/ryan-gosling-fully-immersed-in-blue -valentine.
7. Quoted in Alice Fisher. "The Life of Ryan." *Observer* (London), January 8, 2011. www.guardian.co.uk/film/2011/jan /09/ryan-gosling-blue-valentine-film.
8. Quoted in Lim. "A Heartthrob Finds His Tough-Guy Side."
9. Quoted in Rebecca Winters Keegan. "The Oddball." *Time*, October 4, 2007. www.time.com/time/magazine/article/0 ,9171,1668471,00.html.

Chapter 1: The Road to Disney World

10. Quoted in Keegan. "The Oddball."

11. Quoted in Gaby Wood. "'I Live on Skid Row. You Can't Filter Out Reality There.'" *Observer* (London), February 17, 2007. www.guardian.co.uk/culture/2007/feb/18/awardsand prizes.oscars.

12. Quoted in Lilit Marcus. "In Love with a Real Doll." Beliefnet, no date. www.beliefnet.com/Entertainment/Movies /2007/10/In-Love-With-A-Real-Doll.aspx.

13. Quoted in Brett Martin. "Ryan Gosling." *GQ*, January 23, 2011. http://brettmartin.org/2011/01/ryan-gosling.

14. Quoted in Martin. "Ryan Gosling."

15. Quoted in Dave Karger. "Spotlight on Ryan Gosling." *Entertainment Weekly*, April 20, 2007. www.ew.com/ew /article/0,,20035877,00.html.

16. Quoted in Ruben V. Nepales. "Let's Hear It from Goofy Mr. Gosling." *Philippine Daily Inquirer*, August 4, 2011. http://entertainment.inquirer.net/8153/let%E2%80%99s -hear-it-from-goofy-mr-gosling.

17. Quoted in Brian D. Johnson. "TIFF2011: Red Hot Ryan Gosling." *Maclean's*, September 8, 2011. www2.macleans .ca/2011/09/08/red-hot-ryan.

18. Quoted in Wood. "'I Live on Skid Row.'"

19. Quoted in NPR. "Ryan Gosling."

20. Quoted in Lynn Hirschberg. "Michelle Williams & Ryan Gosling: Heart to Heart." *W*, October 2010. www.wmagazine .com/celebrities/2010/10/michelle_williams_ryan_gosling?pri ntable=true%C3%82%C2%A4tPage=1.

21. Quoted in *Life & Style*. "How Eva Seduced Ryan," January 30, 2012, p. 32.

22. Quoted in Lesley O'Toole. "Ryan Gosling: 'I Think Like a Girl.'" *Independent* (London), October 25, 2011. www .independent.co.uk/arts-entertainment/films/features/ryan -gosling--i-think-like-a-girl-2375346.html.

23. Quoted in Neala Johnson. "Q & A with Ryan Gosling." *Herald Sun* (Melbourne, Australia), August 2, 2007. www .heraldsun.com.au/entertainment/movies/q-a-with-ryan -gosling/story-e6frf9h6-1111114086552.

24. Quoted in NPR. "Ryan Gosling."

25. Quoted in *Huffington Post*. "Young Ryan Gosling Interview: 12-Year-Old Actor Talks *Mickey Mouse Club*." Video. October 23, 2012. www.huffingtonpost.com/2012/10/23/young-ryan-gosling-interview-mickey-mouse-club_n_2005385.html.
26. Quoted in Steve Carell. "Ryan Gosling." *Interview Magazine*, no date. www.interviewmagazine.com/film/ryan-gosling/#page2.
27. Quoted in O'Toole. "Ryan Gosling."
28. Quoted in Carell. "Ryan Gosling."
29. Quoted in Karger. "Spotlight on Ryan Gosling."

Chapter 2: Making a Name for Himself

30. Quoted in Johnson. "Q & A with Ryan Gosling."
31. Quoted in Wood. "'I Live on Skid Row.'"
32. April Snellings. "Monster Kid Corner: *Frankenstein and Me* (1997)." *Rue Morgue*, May 14, 2012. www.rue-morgue.com/2012/05/monster-kid-corner-frankenstein-and-me-1997.
33. Quoted in Snellings. "Monster Kid Corner."
34. Quoted in Jarett Wieselman. "Flashback! Gosling's First *Insider* Interview!" *Insider*.com, June 19, 2012. http://the insider.etonline.com/tv/53261_Ryan_Gosling_Trains_For_Young_Hercules/.
35. Quoted in Jake Hamilton. "*Gangster Squad* Interviews." Video. *Huffington Post*, January 9, 2013. www.huffingtonpost.com/2013/01/09/ryan-gosling-young-hercules_n_2440623.html.
36. Quoted in Johnson. "Q & A with Ryan Gosling."
37. Quoted in Carell. "Ryan Gosling."
38. Quoted in Norman Wilner. "Ryan Gosling: Who Knew the Canuck Charmer Had Such Great Comic Chops?" *Now*, July 28–August 4, 2011. www.nowtoronto.com/movies/story.cfm?content=182002.
39. Quoted in Wilner. "Ryan Gosling."
40. Mick LaSalle. "Gaining Ground/Sport Bridges Racial Divide with a Minimum of Clichés in *Remember the Titans*." *San Francisco Chronicle*, September 29, 2000. www.sfgate.com

/movies/article/Gaining-Ground-Sport-bridges-racial-divide
-with-3237445.php#ixzz2Rs2WqtN7.

41. Jeff Vice. "Film Review: *Remember the Titans.*" *Salt Lake City
(UT) Deseret News*, June 27, 2002. www.deseretnews.com
/article/700002574/Remember-the-Titans.html.

42. Robert Wilonsky. "*Clash of the Titans.*" *Dallas Observer*,
September 28, 2000. www.dallasobserver.com/2000-09-28
/film/clash-of-the-titans.

43. Quoted in Lim. "A Heartthrob Finds His Tough-Guy Side."

Chapter 3: Reinventing Ryan

44. Roger Ebert. "*The Believer.*" Roger Ebert.com, June 14, 2012.
www.rogerebert.com/reviews/the-believer-2002.

45. Peter Travers. "*The Believer.*" *Rolling Stone*, May 19, 2001.
www.rollingstone.com/movies/reviews/the-believer-2001
0101.

46. Quoted in Fisher. "The Life of Ryan."

47. Quoted in Hirschberg. "Michelle Williams & Ryan Gosling."

48. Lim. "A Heartthrob Finds His Tough-Guy Side."

49. Quoted in Carell. "Ryan Gosling."

50. Quoted in Keegan. "The Oddball."

51. Mike Clark. "Standout Performances Lift *Murder by Numbers.*" *USA Today*, April 20, 2002. http://usatoday30.usa
today.com/life/enter/movies/2002/2002-04-19-murder-by
-numbers.htm.

52. Brian Rowe. "The Sandra Bullock Files: *Murder by Numbers*
(2002) Ryan Gosling." Suite101.com, August 25, 2010.
http://suite101.com/article/the-sandra-bullock-files-mur
der-by-numbers-2002-ryan-gosling-a410008.

53. Roger Ebert. "*Murder by Numbers.*" Roger Ebert.com, April
19, 2002. www.rogerebert.com/reviews/murder-by-num
bers-2002.

54. *New York Times*. "Male Bonding on a Rough, Raw Proving
Ground," January 8, 2003. www.nytimes.com/2003/01/08
/movies/film-review-male-bonding-on-a-rough-raw-proving
-ground.html?src=pm.

55. Quoted in Nepales. "Let's Hear It from Goofy Mr. Gosling."

56. Ann Hornaday. "A Tear-Stained *Notebook.*" *Washington Post*, June 25, 2004. www.washingtonpost.com/wp-dyn/articles /A4182-2004Jun24.html.

57. Nick Rogers. "Heroes of the Zeroes: *The Notebook.*" Film Yap, August 5, 2010. www.thefilmyap.com/2010/08/05 /heroes-of-the-zeroes-the-notebook.

58. Quoted in Wood. "'I Live on Skid Row.'"

59. Scott Foundas. "Opposites Attract." *LA Weekly*, August 23, 2006. www.laweekly.com/2006-08-24/film-tv/opposites -attract.

60. Lisa Schwarzbaum. "*Half Nelson* (2006)." *Entertainment Weekly*, August 9, 2006. www.ew.com/ew/article/0,,1224 620,00.html.

61. Quoted in JimmyO. "Int.: Ryan Gosling." Movie News. JoBlo Network, April 18, 2007. www.joblo.com/movie-news/inter view-ryan-gosling.

62. Scott Foundas. "Gosling Fires Up *Fracture.*" *LA Weekly*, April 18, 2007. www.laweekly.com/2007-04-19/film-tv /ryan-gosling-fires-up-fracture.

63. Kenneth Turan, "*Lars and the Real Girl.*" *Los Angeles Times*, October 12, 2007. www.latimes.com/cl-et-lars12oct12,0 ,4899684.story.

64. Quoted in Fisher. "The Life of Ryan."

65. Quoted in James Reed. "Making Their Bones as Fledgling Musicians." *Boston Globe*, October 9, 2009. www.boston .com/ae/music/articles/2009/10/09/actor_ryan_gosling_and _pal_scare_up_a_band.

66. Quoted in Johnson. "TIFF2011."

67. Reed. "Making Their Bones as Fledgling Musicians."

68. Lily Borghi. "Gwyneth Paltrow Sings! Ten Notable Screen Stars Gone Songbird." *West Coast Sound* (blog), *LA Weekly*, July 27, 2010. http://blogs.laweekly.com/westcoastsound /2010/07/ten_notable_screen_stars_gone.php.

69. *Guardian* (Charlottetown, Prince Edward Island, Canada). "Ryan Gosling Says Onscreen Intimacy in *Blue Valentine* 'Just Happened.'"

70. Johnson. "TIFF2011."

71. Quoted in David Eisenberg. "Interview: *The Ides of March*'s Ryan Gosling." Cinema Blend, October 6, 2011. www.cinemablend.com/new/Interview-Ides-March-Ryan-Gosling-27199.html.
72. Quoted in Lim. "A Heartthrob Finds His Tough-Guy Side."
73. Quoted in Coyle. "Gosling at Ease in Every Role Except Movie Star."
74. Quoted in Amy Kaufman. "*How to Catch a Monster*: Ryan Gosling to Make Directorial Debut." *Los Angeles Times*, August 29, 2012. www.latimes.com/entertainment/movies/moviesnow/la-et-mn-ryan-gosling-screenplay-directing-christina-hendricks-20120829,0,5737274.story.
75. Quoted in Johnson. "TIFF2011."

Chapter 4: At Home with Ryan

76. Quoted in Emma Jones. "Ryan Gosling Tells All About the Love of His Life (His Dog, George)." *Independent* (London), January 11, 2013. www.independent.co.uk/arts-entertainment/films/features/ryan-gosling-tells-all-about-the-love-of-his-life-his-dog-george-8448580.html.
77. Quoted in Jones. "Ryan Gosling Tells All About the Love of His Life."
78. Quoted in O'Toole. "Ryan Gosling."
79. Quoted in NPR. "Ryan Gosling."
80. Quoted in Lim. "A Heartthrob Finds His Tough-Guy Side."
81. Quoted in Nepales. "Let's Hear It from Goofy Mr. Gosling."
82. Quoted in Martin. "Ryan Gosling."
83. Quoted in Coyle. "Gosling at Ease in Every Role Except Movie Star."
84. Quoted in Contactmusic.com. "Director Baffled by Gosling/McAdams Romance," December 16, 2006. www.contactmusic.com/news/director-baffled-by-goslingmcadams-romance_1016757.
85. Quoted in *Life & Style*. "How Eva Seduced Ryan," p. 35.
86. Quoted in Tauber. "The Chemistry of Ryan Gosling," p. 66.
87. Quoted in *Life & Style*. "Eva Mendes and Ryan Gosling: Inside Their Whirlwind Relationship," January 18, 2012. www.lifeandstylemag.com/entertainment/news/eva-mendes-and-ryan-gosling-inside-their-whirlwind-relationship.

88. Quoted in Martin. "Ryan Gosling."
89. Quoted in *Mail* Online. "'It Would Have Been Less Trouble to Get Run Over': British Journalist Who Tweeted About Being 'Literally' Saved by Ryan Gosling Fights Against Backlash," April 6, 2012. www.dailymail.co.uk/news /article-2126304/Laurie-Penny-saved-Ryan-Gosling-British -journalist-faces-Twitter-backlash.html.
90. Quoted in Jane Mulkerrins, "Ryan Gosling: I'm Kind of a Girl About Some Things—like Clothes," *Metro* (London), September 21, 2011. http://metro.co.uk/2011/09/21/ryan -gosling-from-crazy-stupid-love-im-kind-of-a-girl-about -some-things-like-clothes-158012.
91. Quoted in Mulkerrins. "Ryan Gosling."
92. Quoted Veronica Boodhan. "Time for Tagine." *Lifestyle*, July 1, 2011. www.lifestylemagazine.ca/tagine_restaurant.

Chapter 5: Ryan's Causes

93. JimmyO. "Int: Ryan Gosling."
94. Quoted in John Prendergast and Don Cheadle. *The Enough Moment: Fighting to End Africa's Worst Human Rights Crimes.* New York: Three Rivers, 2010, pp.157–158.
95. Quoted in Prendergast and Cheadle. *The Enough Moment*, p. 158.
96. Quoted in JimmyO. "Int: Ryan Gosling."
97. Quoted in JimmyO. "Int: Ryan Gosling."
98. Quoted in Karger. "Spotlight on Ryan Gosling."
99. Ryan Gosling and John Prendergast. "Congo's Conflict Minerals: The Next Blood Diamonds." *The Blog, Huffington Post*, April 27, 2011. www.huffingtonpost.com/ryan -gosling/congos-conflict-minerals-_b_854023.html.
100. Quoted in *The PETA Files* (blog). "Ryan Gosling, Our Hero." PETA, September 12, 2011. www.peta.org/b/the petafiles/archive/2011/09/12/ryan-gosling-our-hero.aspx.
101. Ryan Gosling. Letter to Jerry Kozak. Quoted on PETA website, April 1, 2013. www.peta.org/features/ryan -gosling-cow-dehorning-letter.aspx.
102. Quoted in Look to the Stars. "Celebrities Speak Out: Walmart Pork Is Cruelty on a Fork." August 23, 2013.

www.looktothestars.org/news/8831-celebrities-speak-out
-walmart-pork-is-cruelty-on-a-fork.

103. Quoted in Tom Shone. "In the Driving Seat: Interview with
     Ryan Gosling." *Telegraph* (London), September 11, 2011.
     www.telegraph.co.uk/culture/film/film-news/8750070/In-
     the-driving-seat-interview-with-Ryan-Gosling.html.
104. Quoted in O'Toole. "Ryan Gosling."
105. Quoted in NPR. "Ryan Gosling."
106. Quoted in David Ehrlich. "*Blue Valentine* NC-17 Rating
     Reversed; Ryan Gosling Accuses MPAA of Sexism." *Mov-
     iefone*, December 8, 2010. http://blog.moviefone.com
     /2010/12/08/blue-valentine-rating-nc-17.
107. Quoted S.T. VanAirsdale. "Ryan Gosling Tees Off on
     'Misogynistic' MPAA over *Blue Valentine* Rating." *Mov-
     ieline*, November 18, 2010. http://movieline.com/2010
     /11/18/ryan-gosling-tees-off-on-misogynistic-mpaa-over
     -blue-valentine-rating.

1980
Ryan Thomas Gosling is born on November 12 in London, Ontario, Canada.

1981
Moves with his family to Cornwall, Ontario.

1989
Begins entering talent contests and singing at weddings with his sister, Mandi; joins his uncle Perry's Elvis Presley tribute act, called Elvis Perry.

1991–1992
Is homeschooled for a year by his mother.

1993
Auditions for a revival of the *Mickey Mouse Club* and is given a two-year contract; moves to Orlando, Florida, where the show is filmed; his parents' marriage ends in divorce; lives with Justin Timberlake's family for six months.

1995
Returns to Canada after *The All New Mickey Mouse Club* is canceled; appears in episode of *Are You Afraid of the Dark?*

1996
Lands guest spots in episodes of *Psi Factor: Chronicles of the Paranormal*, *Kung Fu: The Legend Continues*, *Road to Avonlea*, *Goosebumps*, *The Adventures of Shirley Holmes*, *Ready or Not*, and *Flash Forward*.

1997
Moves to Burlington, Ontario; drops out of high school to devote himself to acting career; appears in *Frankenstein and Me*; lands a part in a TV series, *Breaker High*.

1998

Appears in the TV movie *Nothing Too Good for a Cowboy*; is cast as the title character on the TV show *Young Hercules* and moves to New Zealand where it is filmed.

1999

Decides not to take any more TV roles and moves to Los Angeles to pursue a career in film; after having trouble landing roles as an adult, he is dropped by his agent.

2000

Appears in the high school football drama *Remember the Titans* with Denzel Washington.

2001

Plays a conflicted Jewish neo-Nazi in *The Believer*.

2002

Appears in *The Slaughter Rule* and *Murder by Numbers*; begins dating costar Sandra Bullock.

2003

Appears in *The United States of Leland*.

2004

Appears opposite Rachel McAdams in the romantic drama *The Notebook*.

2005

Appears in the psychological thriller *Stay*; visits refugee camps in Chad; works as volunteer in Biloxi, Mississippi, to help the cleanup effort after Hurricane Katrina; is arrested on a drunk driving charge in Los Angeles and receives two years' probation; begins dating Rachel McAdams off and on over the next three years.

2006

Plays a drug-addicted high school teacher in *Half Nelson*, a performance that earns him an Oscar nomination for Best Actor.

2007

Appears in *Fracture* and *Lars and the Real Girl*; visits Uganda to help victimized children.

2008

Forms band Dead Man's Bones with Zach Shields and begins recording an album.

2009

Releases debut album, *Dead Man's Bones*; tours North America with band; begins dating Kat Dennings.

2010

Appears in *Blue Valentine* and *All Good Things*; visits eastern Congo; dates Blake Lively.

2011

Appears in *Drive*, *The Ides of March*, and *Crazy, Stupid, Love*; dates Olivia Wilde; begins a long-term relationship with Eva Mendes.

2012

Joins several other celebrities to pen a letter on behalf of animal rights group Mercy for Animals to implore Walmart to stop using suppliers that use inhumane practices in raising pigs.

2013

Appears in *Gangster Squad*, *The Place Beyond the Pines*, and *Only God Forgives*; announces he is taking a hiatus from acting to focus on directing.

2014

Directorial debut, *How to Catch a Monster,* scheduled for release.

For More Information

Books

Don Carter. *Ryan Gosling in the Public Eye*, 2013. Kindle edition. This book contains numerous photos and interviews with Gosling and chronicles his career and personal life.

Danielle Henderson. *Feminist Ryan Gosling: Feminist Theory (as Imagined) from Your Favorite Sensitive Movie Dude*. Philadelphia: Running Press, 2011. The author of this book, a graduate student in gender studies, is the creator of *The Feminist Ryan Gosling* blog. The book contains photos of Gosling paired with witty feminist observations culled from the author's studies.

Nick Johnstone. *Ryan Gosling: Hollywood's Finest*. London: Blake, 2013. This book chronicles Gosling's rise from Mouseketeer to Hollywood heartthrob.

John Prendergast and Don Cheadle. *The Enough Moment: Fighting to End Africa's Worst Human Rights Crimes*. New York: Three Rivers, 2010. Cowritten by human rights activist John Prendergast and actor Don Cheadle, this book details efforts to combat genocide, rape, and other atrocities in Africa. It features a section in which Ryan Gosling discusses his experiences traveling to Chad and Uganda.

Periodicals

Loren King. "Derek Cianfrance Sticks with Ryan Gosling, Again Goes Deep." *Boston Globe*, March 30, 2013.

Dennis Lim. "Myth Making on Motorcycles." *New York Times*, March 22, 2013.

A.O. Scott. "These Law Enforcers Will Stop at Nothing." *New York Times*, January 10, 2013.

Betsy Sharkey. "Ryan Gosling in *The Place Beyond the Pines*: The Eyes Have It." *Los Angeles Times*, April 4, 2013.

Steven Zeitchik. "*Only God Forgives* Trailer Punches Up Gosling Fan Excitement." *Los Angeles Times*, April 4, 2013.

Internet Sources

Monty Archibald. "'They Call Me Mouse Boy!' Ryan Gosling Reveals His Forgotten Nickname in Vintage Mouseketeer Interview." *Mail* Online, October 23, 2012. www.dailymail.co.uk /tvshowbiz/article-2222222/Ryan-Gosling-reveals-forgotten -nickname-vintage-Mouseketeer-interview.html.

David Denby. "Rough Rides." *New Yorker*, April 1, 2013. www .newyorker.com/arts/critics/cinema/2013/04/01/130401crci _cinema_denby.

Scott Foundas. "Is Ryan Gosling Parodying Masculinity?" *LA Weekly*, March 28, 2013. www.laweekly.com/2013-03-28 /film-tv/place-beyond-pines-ryan-gosling.

Tad Friend. "Guy's Guy." *New Yorker*, March 25, 2013. www .newyorker.com/talk/2013/03/25/130325ta_talk_friend.

Ryan Gosling and John Prendergast. "At War in the Fields of the Lord." ABC News, March 1, 2007. http://abcnews.go.com/In ternational/story?id=2915362&page=1#.UXg9rco52sE.

Julie Miller. "Derek Cianfrance on *The Place Beyond the Pines*: 'There Were Many Takes Ruined' by People Staring at Shirtless Ryan Gosling." *The Hollywood Blog, Vanity Fair*, March 26, 2013. www.vanityfair.com/online/oscars/2013/03/ryan-gos ling-the-place-beyond-the-pines-derek-cianfrance-interview.

Julie Miller. "Today in 'Way Too Soon' Casting Rumors: Ryan Gosling and Charlize Theron Courted for Oscar Pistorius Biopic." *The Hollywood Blog, Vanity Fair*, March 27, 2013. www .vanityfair.com/online/oscars/2013/03/ryan-gosling-charlize -theron-oscar-pistorius.

New York Post. "Ryan Gosling: Don't Call Eva Mendes 'Baby,'" April 1, 2013. www.nypost.com/p/pagesix/don_call_mendes _baby_vyLGYMXnsq6jxwS9xfmskO.

New York Times. "Ryan Gosling—About This Person." http:// movies.nytimes.com/person/1548266/Ryan-Gosling.

Maureen O'Connor. "Ryan Gosling Just Isn't That Into You, and You Need to Accept That." *New York*, March 25, 2013. http:// nymag.com/thecut/2013/03/ryan-gosling-just-isnt-that-into -you.html.

Lesley O'Toole. "*Blue Valentine* duo Ryan Gosling and Derek Cianfrance reunited for *The Place Beyond the Pines*." *Independent* (London), April 9, 2013. www.independent.co.uk /arts-entertainment/films/features/blue-valentine-duo-ryan -gosling-and-derek-cianfrance-reunited-for-the-place-be yond-the-pines-8564931.html.

Nick Pinkerton. "*Gangster Squad* Retells the Stories of Better Movies." *LA Weekly*, January 10, 2013. www.laweekly .com/2013-01-10/film-tv/gangster-squad-review.

Dennis Tang. "10 Steps to a Very Ryan Gosling Valentine's Day." *GQ*, February 13, 2013. www.gq.com/entertainment /humor/201302/ryan-gosling-valentines-day#slide=1.

Rebecca Twomey. "Ryan Gosling Exposes Sentimental Side as He Talks About Tattoos." *Marie Claire*, April 25, 2013. www.marieclaire.co.uk/news/celebrity/542311/ryan-gos ling-exposes-sentimental-side-as-he-talks-about-tattoos .html#index=1.

Websites

Dead Man's Bones (www.deadmansbones.net). The official website of Gosling's band features video clips of the band performing songs, as well as clips of interviews with the actor and scenes from his movies.

Gosling Fan (http://goslingfan.com). This website, maintained by two Goslings fans, contains photos, videos, news releases, and an in-depth biography of the actor.

Tagine Beverly Hills (www.taginebeverlyhills.com). The official website of the restaurant co-owned by Ryan Gosling.

The Feminist Ryan Gosling (http://feministryangosling.tumblr .com). Created and maintained by a graduate student in gender studies, this blog containing photos of Ryan Gosling with feminist captions quickly became a fan favorite and spawned a book.

Picture Credits

Cover: © Stephen Lovekin/Getty Images Entertainment/Getty Images

© AP Images/Eric Charbonneau, 48

© AP Photo/Peter Kramer, 43

© Bold Films/The Kobal Collection, 7

© Carousel Productions/Glass, Ben/Newscom, 31

© Dennis MacDonald/Alamy, 22

© Everett Collection/Newscom, 40

© Focus Features/Newscom, 56

© Hunting Lane Films/The Kobal Collection, 8

© Hunting Lane Films/Silverwood Williams/Newscom, 73

© Invisible Children/ZUMA Press/Newscom, 71

© Jeff Kravitz/FilmMagic/Getty Images, 64

© John Lambert Tips Rf/ZUMA Press/Newscom, 12

© The Kobal Collection, 25

© Liz Hedges/Newscom, 36

© Michael Buckner/Getty Images, 55

© Michael Caulfied/WireImage/Getty Images, 17

© New Line/The Kobal Collection, 39

© Noel Vasquez/Getty Images, 44

© PacificCoastNews/Newscom, 53

© Per-Anders Pettersson/Getty Images, 68

© SF photo/Shutterstock.com, 11

© Sylvain Gaboury/FilmMagic/Getty Images, 15

© Theo Wargo/Getty Images, 51

© Tom Meinelt-Jackson Lee, 59

© Tracy Bennett/Disney Enterprises/ZUMA Press/Newscom, 33

© Walt Disney/Bruckheimer Films/The Kobal Collection, 27

© Walt Disney Pictures/The Kobal Collection, 20

© Win McNamee/Getty Images, 69

Cherese Cartlidge holds a bachelor's degree in psychology and a master's degree in education. She has been an author and editor for more than fifteen years and has written numerous books for children and young adults, including biographies of Jane Lynch, Prince Harry, Taylor Swift, and Anne Hathaway. Cartlidge lives in Georgia with her two children.